The Author in London in 1994.

The Silver Samovar
Reminiscences of the Russian Revolution

by Alexander Poliakoff
with Deborah Sacks

Atlantida Press

Moscow   Nottingham

Atlantida Press,
13 Elm Avenue,
Beeston, Nottingham,
England, NG9 1BU.

Atlantida,
Ulitsa Povarskaya 52,
121825, Moscow,
Russia.

ISBN 5-88011-013-3

Printed by Milford Printers, Nottingham, England.

To Ina Poliakoff
wife, mother and friend
1913 – 1992

"I would moreover submit that, in regard to the power of hoarding up impressions, Russian children of my generation passed through a period of genius, as if destiny were loyally trying what it could for them by giving them more than their share, in view of the cataclysm that was to remove completely the world they had known."

Vladimir Nabokov, "Speak, Memory"

I was a good deal younger than Nabokov. In 1917, I was seven; he was eighteen. Nevertheless, I can conjure to my inner eye the world that disappeared, as easily as if it had been yesterday.

Swiftly, our Moscow lifestyle was effaced - our flat in Manege Square, requisitioned, and the open house, the constant flow of guests, who arrived without warning and stayed to dinner as a matter of course, transfigured to winter isolation.

Yet we were fortunate. Although we were threatened by brigands and eviction by the authorities and although, for a time, we had little to eat, we lived with servants in our well furnished dacha for seven years. Others suffered far more, both in Russia and abroad.

Russians are well known for cherishing their past. I was not quite fourteen when I left and did not return to Russia for forty-two years but the culture still exercises a profound influence on me. No matter how long I have been away or how much English association I have had, such things are not to be forgotten.

A. P. 1994

Editor's Foreword

My father Alexander Poliakoff had been promising to write his memoirs for as long I can remember. In 1994, he finally succeeded with the help of Deborah Sacks. She deserves all our gratitude for patiently coaxing out a manuscript after the rest of us had failed for so long. Once finished, the Silver Samovar was quickly translated into Russian by Larissa Vasilieva, a longstanding friend of the family, and her son Yegor. Larissa's newly formed Moscow cooperative *Atlantida* (Atlantis in English) then published the "Poliakoff Family" as their first book. The volume contained both the Silver Samovar and selected extracts from Zinaida Poliakoff's diary, together with an amusing introduction by Larissa. Sadly, my father was not well enough to go to Moscow for the launch in November 1995 so Mouma's daughter Betka, my sister Miranda and I went in his place. Fortunately, the three of us have retained enough of our heritage to make short speeches in Russian; mine was laced with archaic idioms imperfectly learned from my Grandmother. The book was received with heart-warming enthusiasm and we all felt that our family had made its spiritual return to Russia. Now, the final piece of the jigsaw is about to fall into place. Larissa has just told me that a museum is opening in Mamontovka, where my father lived after the Revolution, with a display devoted to the Poliakoff family.

After our return from the launch in Moscow, an inspired suggestion by Colonel B. D. Shaw (the legendary lecturer on explosives) has led to our publishing an English version in Nottingham under the Atlantida imprint. Finally, I must express our family's thanks to Deborah Sacks and Larissa Vasilieva for their sustained enthusiasm and hard work, to Molly Griffiths for retyping parts of the manuscript, to Chris Salter of Blackwell's University Bookshop and to The Sherwood Press for their help.

Martyn Poliakoff
Nottingham, May 1996.

Chapters

List of illustrations:

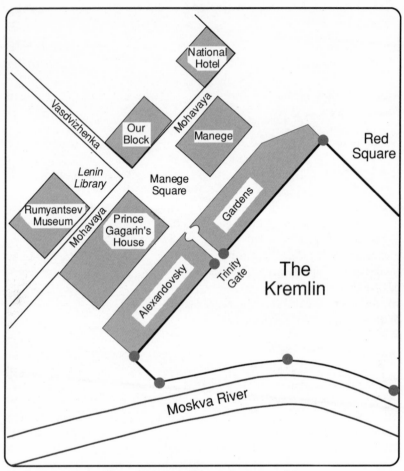

Map of Manege Square (not to scale)

The Manege Square photographed by my daughter-in-law Janet during our visit to Moscow in 1970. The picture was taken from outside the Kremlin gate. The facade of the Manege is on the right, "our block" is straight ahead and the start of Vasdvizhenka is in the distance on the left. Our flat was on the first floor, the "Belle Etage" as it was called then. Our windows are the first seven from the left.

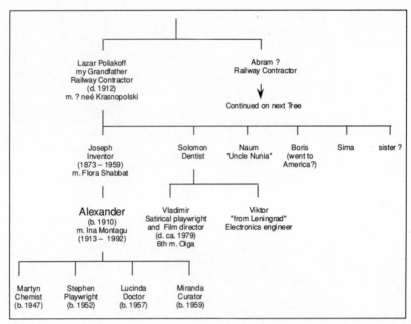

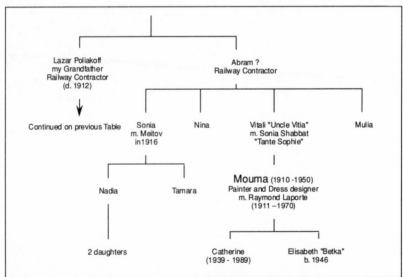

The Poliakoff Family

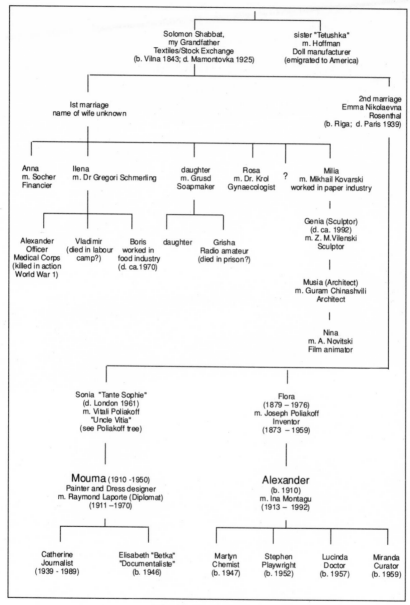

The Shabbat Family

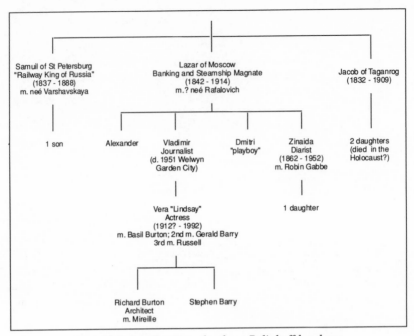

Grandfather's Cousins, the three Poliakoff brothers.

The October Revolution

I used to look out through my nursery window and see the gilt onion domes of the Kremlin churches glistening in the sunshine. Behind a low white tower rose the high pinnacle of the Trinity Gate. This housed a clock and sometimes tiny figures could be seen crawling up its steep sides to repair the turret. Above the crenelated walls of the Kremlin rose the domes of the cathedrals and churches dominated by the bell tower of Ivan the Great. Palace buildings of different ages could be seen above the walls and at their base stretched the Alexandrovsky Gardens.

I was in my nursery in bed, suffering slightly from the 'flu when I heard some disturbance in the square. I stood up in bed to get a view of the entire square and saw a rather corpulent officer and two or three cadets or *junkers* running out of the Manege building, pushing a field gun. They stopped in the middle of the square, turned the gun round to the right and fired straight into the Trinity Gate of the Kremlin, which was directly opposite our block. As a result some of our windows flew open and my governess rushed into my nursery followed by my parents. I was pushed in my bed into the dining room which faced the courtyard. The shooting increased in intensity and all the family collected in the dining room.

That, for us, was the start of the October Revolution. The room in which we were to spend a week was unashamedly opulent. All the furniture was made of black oak. Facing me, as I lay in bed, was the main sideboard, surmounted by a large mirror under a classical architrave. The two display cabinets attached to it were filled mainly with silver gilt champagne goblets. A large silver samovar was displayed on a small table on the right. The vast dining table was lit by an electrolier, similar examples of which can still be seen in some suites of the Moscow National Hotel. Its bulbs facing up, down and horizontally could be switched on row by row. Above the other sideboard stood portraits of my maternal grandparents when young, and on the sideboard itself were two porcelain vases, about one foot high, made by Popov at the beginning of the nineteenth century.

The days were cheerful in spite of the sound of shells bursting and machine gun fire but the nights were terrifying. My parents, grandparents, governess and I slept in the dining room while the servants kept to their quarters which faced the courtyard. The front door bell used to ring more than once during the night and we would be accused by one side or the other of showing a light, which we were not, and threatened with dire consequences if we continued. From time to time the servants would rush in, having picked up gossip on the servants' stairs, known in Russia as "the black way". Generally their news was that the Bolsheviks were about to arrive and we were all to have our throats cut. The only person on whom this seemed to make any impression was my grandmother who would then get out of bed repeating, "What will be, will be."

Apart from living in the dining room with the family's beds standing around the wall, life went on as normal and was quite amusing. Our meals appeared as usual and the only difference was that I ate with the grown-ups instead of separately with my governess. My father organised a volunteer defence force, armed with sporting guns, to guard the various entrances to the block and to the courtyard. He worked out the rota and inspected the men at night. Realising that many people in the smaller flats in the block would run out of food, he arranged for the larger households to feed two people each. I remember nothing of the two people allocated to us but have a very clear recollection of the three officers from the Manege who came to dinner every night complete with a balalaika. They sang gypsy romances and folk songs after dinner, before returning to shoot it out with the Bolsheviks who were concentrated in the Kremlin.

Our flat, which was one of the best in the block, was on the first floor. Across the landing from us, lived an old man who had a large beard and wore a blue suit. I have no idea what he did, if he did anything, but he was a believer and he said that he felt no need to shelter in the back of his flat because if God willed him to be shot, then he would be shot and if God willed otherwise, no harm could come to him. Who was he to make the judgment himself? We did not see much of this neighbour generally and I think it was only the shooting that prompted him to make contact.

Then one evening, a sizable shell hit our block a few floors above. The servants rushed in shouting that the building was on fire. In fact the building was not on fire but part of the wall had gone, exposing someone's study to public view. You could see the desk and bookcase from the street, as if you were looking into a doll's house. My father evacuated us to a small hotel in the courtyard and Uncle Vitia, Aunt Sonia and my cousin Mouma, who lived nearby, managed to join us with their servants. We had only one room with a single bed and our servants quickly decided that they preferred the shells to being crowded in with us and went back to the flat. That night, the shooting was the heaviest we had heard. There was no question of sleep. The corridors of the hotel were full of men wearing bowler hats discussing the situation, although in reality nobody knew a thing. In the morning we learnt that the anti-Bolshevik forces had surrendered and we went back to our flat but we had no idea whether they had surrendered just then or during the night. Amazingly, dinner that evening was quite cheerful. The three officers came for dinner without their epaulettes and without the balalaika but they did not seem unduly depressed.

The next day a Captain Dyakanov, whom I had never seen before, arrived with his very beautiful Polish wife and asked for shelter. The Revolution had left them homeless and they were given the English sitting room to live in and remained with us for over six months. Dyakanov had only the slightest connection with my family. He had invented a shell holder, to be made in Father's factory, that screwed on to the barrel of a rifle, so that when the gun was fired, the shell was pushed in the same direction as the bullet. Dyakanov was a cheerful character. As he was on the run, he decided to change to mufti and Father gave him one of his suits. The suit fitted Dyakanov reasonably well but Father had to teach him to tie a tie because, being a Russian officer, he had never worn one.

In a day or two, I was judged well enough to go for a walk and my governess and I emerged to Manege Square. Never before had I seen such a crowd. There were rough looking men wandering about aimlessly, peasants in their sheepskin coats not normally seen in that part of Moscow and many bearded creatures who might have been workers from factories that had closed down or Muscovites who had come to the centre to see what they could get. There were no well dressed people to be seen. Not far away, we saw two houses which were smoking ruins and the sight of them upset me still further. Things I had regarded as permanent had proven to be not permanent at all. It was discouraging and I was anxious to get back to the safety of the flat.

A few days later my parents, my governess and I went to Zagorsk, a famous monastery town seventy kilometres from Moscow. Father's brother, Uncle Nunia, went ahead to arrange our rooms in a hotel meant for pilgrims. We had dinner in an ornate dining room which was full of people like us, who had left Moscow to be out of the way in case of trouble. In between the guest rooms on each floor, there was a room labelled *mujikskaya*, or peasant's room. A *mujik* is a peasant. So there were various expressions. People said, "Once a *mujik* always a *mujik*," or if someone did not behave well they said, "Well he's a *mujik*," which was quite unjust to the peasants. I looked into one of these rooms and saw a large number of bearded men sitting around a table drinking tea. The room I shared with my governess was small and miserable and afforded me no amusement. There was nothing to do in Zagorsk except visit the monastery. However I was very impressed by the monks' refectory, which appeared to be panelled in gold. Fifty years later I revisited Zagorsk but found the refectory closed.

The next day Father's friend, Colonel Gardenin, telephoned to invite us to dinner. He was still in command of his regiment stationed in Zagorsk and we were fetched and brought back by a military coachman in a sleigh and pair. When Father tipped him, the soldier drew himself up and replied with the usual, "*Rad staratsa*," meaning 'pleased to serve'. Things had not changed yet. At the Colonel's house there was a large dinner party. His two daughters and I had our meal separately with our two governesses and were then put on chamber pots in a line. One of the girls was my age, the other two years older. The older girl eventually married the Ambassador of Monaco in Paris. Twenty years later, I met these girls on my honeymoon in Monte Carlo and reminded them of our first meeting, including the pots.

Two or three weeks later we returned to Moscow. As usual the flat was full of guests and family and there was a large dinner party. My cousin Mouma sat with a large bow in her hair and listened to my account of everything I had seen in Zagorsk, while Captain Dyakanov told stories of his exploits in the army. Nothing at home had changed. Our pretty parlour maid, Polya, was at the front door. Luba, our cook, was in the kitchen. Adam, our manservant, served at dinner. The Dyakanovs were still living in the English sitting room. I was happy to be back to the world I was used to - my large nursery full of toys, the gardens of the Rumyantsev Museum and the children I played with there.

Life appeared to go an as normal and at lunch time and in the evenings there were always guests. The nights however were still unpleasant. A feeling of insecurity remained and there were occasional bouts of shooting. Once during the firing, Captain Dyakanov found himself in the Kremlin Palace and pushed his revolver and gold watch into a cavity in one of the walls. Incredibly, he was let through the next morning and was able to recover both and display them at lunch.

One night my parents went out to a dinner party and for some reason my governess disappeared after putting me to bed. The shooting started in earnest and I was convinced that my parents would be killed. I became more and more alarmed and started crying bitterly. Then the door opened and Dyakanov's tall, gracious wife came in. I was thrilled and excited because although only seven, I was already in love with her. She was wearing her dressing gown and her hair was in long plaits. We spent a quarter of an hour kissing each other and she dried my tears and stayed with me until my parents returned quite late.

My parents were acquainted with a "first nighter," someone who felt he had to be at every opening in Moscow. He was friendly with a well-known tenor called Sobinov who lived in our block of flats and he used to visit us quite frequently. Very soon after the October Revolution, he came to dinner in a state of great excitement because the previous night he had been at the Bolshoi Theatre when for the first time, high-ranking commissars had occupied the Royal Box. In those days you were not obliged to take off your galoshes before going into the theatre. So when the commissars appeared, all the men in the audience who were wearing galoshes took them off and bombarded the commissars in their Royal Box. The doors were locked and the police arrived and searched the audience for weapons. Our "first nighter" hid his revolver under his fur hat and in the hurry of searching it was not discovered. Appearing in the Royal Box was tactless and unnecessary. It did not give the best view because it was too far away from the stage and its function was purely ceremonial having rooms behind to dine and entertain guests.

Manege Square

Our flat was in a large block on the corner of Mohovaya and Vasdvizhenka. Mohovaya went from Manege Square towards the old university, the National Hotel and the Bolshoi Theatre. The frontage of our block was on Manege Square but our main entrance was in Vasdvizhenka. We could go by lift which was operated by a porter from his lodge but normally we took the stairs. It was an old block and originally there had been no lift so I suppose, living on the first floor as we did, gave the more prosperous tenants as much exercise as they were thought to require. Now the entrance is blocked by the Metro station so you have to go through the ground floor of Kalinin's Reception and up an internal staircase to reach our flat.

Coming in through the front door, one arrived in the marble-floored hall. Straight ahead was the dining room. To the left was the English sitting room and to the right was the main reception room, known as the study. The principal rooms of the flat faced the square while the English sitting room, the dining room and the servants' quarters faced the court. As far as we were concerned we were living quite comfortably but in truth it was an extremely inconvenient flat. Most of the rooms had large double doors three-quarters of the way into the room, opposite each other to the left and right of the room, as in French flats of that period. These enabled the flat to be opened up to form a vast space for parties but the lack of a central hallway created a one way system. The double doors in the study gave the only access to my grandparents' room. Similarly, you had to go through the dining room to get to the bathroom and lavatory. The only other way would have been to go out through the front door, down to Vasdvizhenka Street, turn right into the courtyard, go up the servants' staircase and through the kitchen and servants' corridor. Of course no one made this journey and chamber pots were used as in most places. I remember once being taken to the lavatory with Mouma by our respective nannies. Instead of waiting for me to finish, Mouma's nanny lifted Mouma to relieve herself into the wash basin. Even then, I thought this was a little eccentric.

The flat was heated by huge Dutch stoves that went from floor to ceiling and were very wide. The stoves to heat the hall and the study were fired from the hall and were decorated with terracotta or stone. The stoves had to be lit very early in the morning and kept going with birch logs until evening. Then the blue flame disappeared and the chimneys were shut to store the heat till the following morning. The stoves warmed the place more evenly than the open fires used in England and France but they required a great deal of labour like all things in old Russia.

At regular intervals, two men known as *polateri* (meaning floor rubbers) used to come. They put material with polish under their feet, rolled up the carpets and the ballet would begin. They danced and danced until the floors gleamed in every room and their small spectator had grown dizzy with watching.

Everybody noticed our parlour maid, the fair-haired, blue-eyed Polya. In Tsarist Russia guests would tip the servants as they showed them out and Polya was supposed to get very good tips. She had a sweet character as well as being very pretty. She came from a peasant family and it would have been considered a tremendous rise in the world for her to go into town, to eat altogether superior food and to be dressed, when she went out, in almost Western styles. We had a change of manservant around the time of the First Revolution. I am not sure exactly when Adam arrived but he was certainly installed by the time of the October Revolution. The first manservant was a Latvian and my only memory of him is of driving, in a horse cab, with him and Polya. This was unusual because normally I would have travelled with my governess. I rarely came across our cook Luba. She was married to a railway worker named Trofim who appeared occasionally. I only remember visiting the servants' quarters once. The kitchen was very large with a free standing stove in the middle of the room. There was a separate room for the maidservants but the unfortunate Adam had to sleep on a shelf in the corridor.

Out of the blue "the little uncle" arrived in Moscow. He was Grandfather's brother who had disappeared leaving his wife and two children to do the best they could in Vilna. He was given the small English sitting room to sleep in. He was very tidy. He had a grey military moustache and dressed in a neat grey suit. His grown children, who lived in Moscow, came to see him. Then he disappeared again.

There were guests at every meal. People would arrive unannounced, dine if it was a suitable hour and then sit till two in the morning without worrying that the host might want to get rid of them. So the social life was continuous and far greater than in the West. Virtually all the prosperous households were open houses and people just wandered in and had meals. If it was not meal time then they would stay for lunch or dinner or both, and there was no nonsense about warning people you were coming. You just arrived and were naturally asked to stay. I think this is what is meant by the expression "the wide Russian soul." I once read an article written by a journalist who was considering whether to emigrate. On the positive side of living in Russia, he said, "Where else could I wake up my friend at two o'clock in the morning to complain about my wife?" He could not conceive that such a thing would be welcome elsewhere.

I did not participate in this social life but ate my meals in the dining room before the table had been laid for my parents and their guests. It was not until we were in the country, between the two Revolutions, that I ate with the adults. However I was present at a lunch in 1916 when a director of Marconi arrived from London with his wife, sister-in-law and a little girl called Margot. Totally uninhibited by foreign surroundings, Margot chattered away endlessly in English which of course I did not understand. I found the whole thing amazing: a child speaking without first being addressed, as strange as the language she spoke.

I used to breakfast in the dining room with my nanny or governess. I had white bread, saltless butter and caviar for breakfast every day. I may have had cocoa to drink. I do not know whether my parents had the same because I never saw them eat breakfast but I was supposed to be a delicate child and my diet was supervised by my doctor, Shapiro, so presumably that was the approved breakfast. I had a light lunch, generally *pojarski* cutlets (minced chicken or veal cooked in sour cream) followed by *kissyel*, a translucent dessert made from cranberries or red currants and sugar. After my lunch I was supposed to rest so I went to lie on top of my bed and told myself stories. I had a collection of whips and things to twiddle (all male Poliakoffs like fiddling with things) and I remember particularly the full sized white leather whip of the Berlin coachman which I was given for my third birthday. I was very happy to be there alone telling myself stories until it was time for me to get up. Then I was given supper which was again *pojarski* cutlets and *kissyel*. I do not think it ever varied.

After breakfast I would play in my nursery. My favourite toy was a scale model of the Moscow cab sleigh complete with a pair of rocking horses. Two children or one adult could be carried in its passenger seat but generally I played alone, making the noise of the horses' hoofs as I rode. I also had a large circus tent, which like many of my toys, Father had bought for me in England. There were painted wooden clowns with flexible joints, animals, trapezes and all sorts of apparatus and I spent hours arranging things inside and outside the tent.

I remember no lessons as such before the Revolution but my governess must have taught me to read and write and I would recite the Russian nursery rhymes:

Little Sparrow where have you been
Drinking Vodka on Fantanka Street
I had a glass and then another
And a noise started in my head.

Why are there no hot macaronis on Mount Ararat?
Because Napoleon made war in Arbat Street.

With Marie, my first governess, I used to walk through the Trinity Gate to the Kremlin to admire the Tsar Gun and the Tsar Bell, an enormous damaged church bell just inside the entrance. Once when I was walking with my governess, I saw a number of convicts, escorted by police, with chains between their legs. We would walk to the grounds of the Rumyantsev Museum to play with other children, all of whom were also accompanied by a nanny or governess. The grounds were well timbered and there was an old tree, with a large hollow, in which we used to hide things. We played hide and seek and other games approved by our governesses as suitable for well bred children. Our playground has now gone and the Lenin library stands in its place.

The Moscow beggars did not pursue you like those in the East and in our part of town they were fairly rare. But they were terrifying when they did appear, having either no legs or no arms and large matted beards. I never allowed my governess to get near enough to give them any money. I was a very self-controlled child, not open at all and I would never admit to being frightened but I used to say to my governess, "I'm cold, don't you think we'd better go home?" I remember one occasion when I said something like this and she replied, "Where's the beggar then?" because she was used to me making excuses.

There was a toboggan run at the Hunter's Club, now the Kremlin Hospital, a few doors away from the entrance to our block of flats, in Vasdvizhenka Street. When I was five, my maternal grandfather took me to buy a toboggan. We went to what is now GUM, the State Universal Store in Red Square, the largest of the Soviet department stores. In those days it was called *Torgovy Ryad*, literally Trade Row, and consisted of a large number of small shops on several levels selling every conceivable thing. In front of each shop, in the passageways, sat large bearded merchants in semi-peasant dress on the look out for customers. Grandfather and I went into one such shop and picked out a prize toboggan. It had a metal chassis and runners and fabric printed with violets. Grandfather did not haggle but told the merchant that he never bought anything without a discount of ten percent. The merchant was tall and dressed in black with a Russian shirt and a long grey beard. He deliberated for a while, then sold Grandfather the toboggan.

I did not see a great deal of my mother before the Revolution. She made an effort to read to me a couple of times a week but unfortunately did not realise that the book was well above my head and I was too well behaved to mention it. Occasionally I saw her being made ready to go out to dinner or to the theatre when Polya used to wave her hair with heated tongs. Mother had no interest in clothes and Father chose most of her wardrobe, asking girls with Mother's measurements to model dresses when he went abroad.

9

Long before the Revolution, Manege Square had become a source of entertainment to me. On one occasion I saw Tsar Nicholas II arrive in military uniform for an inspection in the Manege. On Saint Tatiana's Day, I watched the students celebrating, with the secret police hovering nearby. After the secret police had been pointed out to me, I could spot them myself because whenever a group formed, they would walk up to it. Students were always giving trouble and they were carefully watched - on Saint Tatiana's day in particular because she was their patron saint and they considered it a propitious day to demonstrate or conspire. Most of the traffic in Moscow was horse-drawn and I loved to watch the beautifully polished private carriages with horses, often in matching pairs, driven by coachmen in long, heavily padded blue robes, red sashes and hard hats like the headgear worn by Churchill. The few cars there were all looked different because they had individually made bodies displaying unique accessories: enormous brass acetylene headlights and fancy horns with squeeze rubber bulbs. I found the Manege drunks amusing. Once I saw a well-dressed man, in a dark coat and bowler hat, on his knees in the middle of the square arranging pieces of brocade cloth as though he intended to carpet the whole square. A couple of policeman were remonstrating with him and eventually led him away.

Like many Russian Jews born in the two capitals, I was brought up in a completely assimilated manner. I did not learn Hebrew or go to synagogue and the family celebrated Christmas and Easter in a manner indistinguishable from Orthodox Christians. We did not go to church but by that time only the peasants and the aristocracy did. In the eyes of the Russian intelligentsia, the church was an accomplice of the Tsarist regime. Jews who adopted Christianity, however formally, immediately became free of all legal restrictions and limitations. Yet in spite of our indifference to matters of religion, there was never any question of us converting. The challenge was to manage nevertheless to do everything the Jews were not allowed to do. To have been baptised would have been unsporting.

On walks with Marie I used to cross myself as we passed churches with icons outside. On more than one occasion Marie said, "It is not necessary for you to cross yourself" and, puzzled by this remark, I would reply, "But everyone crosses themselves; why shouldn't I?" Marie never answered my question. Then one day I asked my grandfather why we did not go to church and he told me it was because we were Jews.

"Am I a Jew?"

"Yes, Shura, you are".

I did not know what a Jew was but thought it was an amusing thing to be and rushed from the room to impart the glad tidings to whomever would listen. I bumped into my Uncle Vitia and said, "Uncle, I am a Jew but you are not because you come from Petrograd." My uncle roared with laughter and went off to tell my grandparents that from now on he was a gentile. Clearly, I thought that to be a Jew one had to live in Manege Square, or at least in Moscow.

I think it was in the autumn of 1915 that the square filled with cars. All motor vehicles in Moscow were to be inspected outside the Manege and if suitable, requisitioned for the front. From early morning, I was glued to the windows, dashing away only to drag Marie to share the spectacle with me. The variety of cars was enormous. At the time I was unable to distinguish the makes but recognized the one used by the Tsar, a Delaune Belleville, by its circular radiator. Then Father came into my nursery and offered to take me to the inspection in our car. There was a shortage of petrol so Father and the driver started the car on kerosene and with the engine coughing and spluttering, we drove the fifty or so yards to the entrance of the Manege. We waited our turn to be inspected. Then three men lifted the bonnet and Father and the driver got out. After a brief conversation among themselves, the three uniformed men rejected our car as insufficiently powerful for military requirements and we drove home.

Apart from this outing, my war work consisted entirely of scrawling my name at the end of letters that Marie or Mother sent on my behalf to half a dozen soldiers with parcels of cigarettes, socks and chocolate. One of the soldiers was a Cossack and his letters were written in the flowery language typical of people from the south, "Light of my heart, I embrace you. The beautiful socks were very useful but please send more cigarettes. May God bless you and all your dear family, and may you grow up as strong as a Cossack." My cousin, Alexander Schmerling, appeared looking handsome and unfamiliar in the uniform of an officer in the Medical Corps but otherwise nothing changed in my well regulated life.

In the Summer of 1916, when we were staying in a dacha in Sokolniki, there was an anti-German pogrom in Moscow because of the war. German pianos were thrown out of windows and shops with German names were damaged, including Einem, the principal chocolate shop in *Kusnetski Most*, the Bond Street of Moscow. On that day, my father's cousin, Sonia Poliakoff, had chosen to be married although, of course, she did not have advance notice of the pogrom. The wedding was held in our flat in Manege Square and my parents went ahead to oversee the preparations. I arrived with my governess in a hired car. The double doors in most rooms had been opened and I was amazed to see pale blue hydrangeas and little palm trees all over the flat. When I looked out of my nursery, I saw a man in a straw hat. I thought, "That's very odd. Why is he wearing a hat indoors?" So I asked someone about it and was told he was the rabbi who was going to marry the happy couple. I was not a guest at the wedding and did not see the ceremony, only the man in the straw hat, so it is unclear why I was brought to town.

Sonia was not particularly young and she married a man called Meitov. They both used to come and see us at the dacha. He was incredibly lazy and would not join in any games, whether croquet or anything else and never wanted to go for walks. But in spite of his laziness he was supposed to be very rich.

About this time I befriended a little girl called Beba. She lived only a short distance from us and I remember going to her birthday party in a very long reception room full of her relations in military uniform. It was probably my first invitation, for usually only adults were invited to children's birthday parties. However, Beba's interest in me was by no means constant and there were times when I felt very neglected by her.

*　　*　　*

New Year's Eve was always celebrated at home. Additional tables were put in the dining room and places were laid for about sixty people. The flat hummed with activity. At my usual bedtime, with the noise of people arriving, I said my prayers on my knees and Marie put me to bed. My prayers were formal petitions to God to look after my parents, my grandparents and Marie. I suppose Marie thought that the servants were under God's special protection and did not need my pleading. A few minutes after midnight my father would come in with a golden goblet in his hand, wake me up, kiss me and touch the champagne to my lips.

That midnight visit apart, he was quite a remote figure. He was frequently abroad for long periods and since I did not see him at meal times, our contact was limited to his occasional visits to my nursery. I saw more of him when we travelled abroad. In 1913 we went to Switzerland, to Wildungen, a German watering place and finally to Berlin. I remember sampling the water in Wildungen in a blue glass with something written on it in gold letters but as far as I remember the water had a bitter taste and failed to please me. Also in Wildungen, I had an encounter with a Grand Duke which I do not remember but which my parents were fond of recounting. I was with my nanny at the place where people collected their glass of water. She was dressed in the uniform of a Russian nanny and the Grand Duke walked up to us, patted me on my head and said, "What a beautiful Russian child." I celebrated my third birthday in a hotel in Berlin and went to a zoo where a chimpanzee was riding a tricycle among the visitors. Then I remember arriving back in Moscow and being met by Genia, Mother's niece, who was much older than me. She was wearing a small hat with a little veil and she carried a modest bouquet of red roses and a sign saying, "Welcome Back to Moscow."

I seldom went out with my father and remember only four occasions in pre-Revolutionary Moscow. The first was when Father took me to the

Moscow zoo. We were accompanied by my governess Marie. Curiously, I remember nothing of the zoo but have the clearest recollection of the return journey. For some reason our car was not available and we had taken a horse cab to the zoo. When we came out, there were no cabs and, though we waited, none came. It was getting cold. Trams kept passing but Father had no intention of exposing his child to the interior of a tram. Eventually, he boarded a tram from the exit at the front and tipped the driver to allow us to stand next to him as far as was necessary to find a cab.

Another outing was with a man called Mr Williamson from the English company, Marconi. We travelled in a hired landau with a pair of horses to Sokolniki, a spacious park just outside Moscow. The men attempted to play golf on one of the football grounds but were largely frustrated by village boys who chased after the balls and brought them back. Marie and I also accompanied Father to try his special binoculars by the Moskva river. When he was in London just before the war, someone had challenged him to invent a device to make it easier to see submarine periscopes in choppy seas. He went to Negretti & Zambra Instrument Makers and ordered binoculars with the image in one eye inverted. He thought that the movement of the sea would thus be cancelled in the brain so that the waves would be perceived as stationary by the viewer. Unfortunately, the water did not obligingly move just up and down and the binoculars only succeeded in giving the user a considerable headache. When he collected the binoculars, the manager of the Regent Street showroom came out and asked Father what the idea was. Without blinking an eye, Father replied, "When I go to the Alhambra, I want to see the girls upright and upside down!" At that time the Alhambra was the best known music hall in Leicester Square.

Father's laboratory was more or less opposite my mother's birthplace in *Miasnitskaya*, later called Kirov Street. Father only took me there once. A porter took us up in a hydraulic lift which impressed me greatly because I thought he was pulling us up by the rope unaided by any hydraulics. Father's laboratory was large and very tidy. He summoned an assistant who made some adjustments and very bright lights started flashing on the apparatus but I received no explanation which I could understand about what he was investigating. This was the only occasion that Father took me out without Marie.

At this stage, I respected and admired Father but had no chance to develop the real affection which came a good deal later. However there was a lot to admire in this handsome figure, impeccably dressed and obviously looked up to by everyone around him. His attitude to me, his only child, would not have met with the approval of modern educationalists. My aunt Sonia, when staying with us in London after the war said, "The Revolution saved you, for you were brought up like the Prince of Wales but you were not the Prince of Wales." Like all the Poliakoffs, I was made to feel that there was something special about me. At the same time, I was in no way spoiled. I never argued with my parents or governess and very rarely complained.

Approximately a year before the Revolution, Marie, my governess from the Baltic provinces was replaced by Jeanne, a French speaking governess from Switzerland. Jeanne had trained as an opera singer and, when she was interviewed, I was asked into the room to sing something in French while Father accompanied me on the piano. I was accustomed to applause after such a performance but Jeanne did not clap because I had sung out of tune. Despite this inauspicious start, I grew very attached to her and when she was repatriated, roughly nine months after the Revolution, I remember standing up in bed, in floods of tears, and her calling, "Au revoir, mon petit, au revoir."

*   *   *

The February Revolution which resulted in the Tsar's abdication and the installation of the Provisional Government was a pageant of what later became known as "people's power." I was playing in my nursery just after breakfast when about fifty mounted gendarmes rode into the Manege. The servants rushed in to watch from my window as the gates of the Manege were shut and guards were posted all around the building. No sooner was this accomplished than a vast crowd arrived in the square, led by a student holding what looked like a toy sword high above his head. The sword was tied with a large red ribbon.

The crowd began persuading the guards to join them one by one. People detached themselves from the crowd and walked up to the guards; three or four people tackled each soldier and we could see the guards as they walked across to join the crowd. Of course we could not see what was happening on the other side of the Manege. Whenever a soldier yielded, we saw the people cheering but we could not hear anything because it was February and the closed double windows insulated us from sound. Eventually no guards were left and there was a moment of great suspense while we waited to see whether the mounted gendarmes inside the Manege would charge the crowd. This had happened before in many places and on many occasions. But no, the gates opened and the gendarmes rode out led by the head gendarme on a white horse. He unsheathed his sword to reveal that it was tied with a red ribbon. Our servants wondered where he had found the ribbon. They concluded, "He must have brought it with him just in case."

Then, as now, there were only three buildings on Manege Square. The long low Empire-style building was the Manege, a monument built to celebrate Russia's victory against Napoleon in 1812. Its spacious hall was used for horse riding, military parades and exhibitions. Our block of flats occupied the whole side of the square facing the Kremlin and at right angles to this was another block of flats known as Prince Gagarin's house. Many years later, at an Anglo-Russian lunch in London, I was describing this scene when an unassuming man sitting a few places away from me intervened. Prince Gagarin, for it was he, surprised me by saying that I was not the only child to see the First Revolution in the square. He had watched it too with the old prince, his grandfather, from a balcony in their block. Since it was February, they must have been somewhat cold.

For the next few days there was a feeling of joy all over the city. I felt it very strongly even as a child of six. When I returned to Russia, nearly fifty years later, I spoke to an old lady in a museum about the First Revolution and she said, "Do you remember the joy that we all felt? And then it all went."

My Shabbat Grandparents

I never knew my Poliakoff grandparents but, with the exception of a very short period after the Revolution, my maternal grandparents, Solomon and Emma Shabbat, always lived with us. My grandfather, Solomon Shabbat, was born in Vilna, then the capital of Lithuania, in 1843. The Lithuanian Jews were hardworking, sober, good family men and Grandfather was an uncomplicated character whose first aim in life was to provide for his wife and children.

Solomon Shabbat's father was a prosperous textile merchant specialising in suit cloth and when he was fifteen Grandfather went on his first business trip to Moscow. At that time it was very difficult for Jews to get permission to go to Moscow. The few who went there on business, all lodged in the same inn, the *Glebovskoye Podvorye*, located in the centre of the market quarter and went in convoy with guards to each business appointment. In 1859, Alexander II granted the right of residence to selected groups of "useful Jews" including wealthy merchants. As a result of this, Solomon Shabbat gained permission to live in Moscow when he was quite young and was one of the first Jews to settle there. By the time the restrictions were tightened up under Alexander III and Jews were expelled, he was already a Merchant of the First Guild which automatically gave him right of residence.

The only member of my family who had to leave Moscow when the Jews were expelled in 1891 was Grandfather's sister known to us as *tetushka*, meaning "little aunt." Tetushka was married to a man named Hoffman and they moved to the United States. By the time my papa visited America, her husband had established a factory for making dolls. But when the dolls were dispatched to hot parts of the States, their faces used to melt. So she said to Father, "You are an inventor. Do something about it." Father devised a gelatine-based formula that gave flexibility to the dolls faces and survived the heat.

Like all Eastern European Jews of his time, Grandfather married very young, at the age of fifteen or sixteen. He had six daughters by his first marriage. My grandmother, Emma, was Grandfather's second wife. She came from Riga in the Baltic, hundreds of miles from Moscow, so the marriage must have been arranged by a marriage broker after Grandfather's first wife died. I think Grandmother had been left on the shelf for she was not young when she married Grandfather and he was her first husband. I believe she brought almost no dowry. My grandparents did not make an ideal couple. Grandfather was very easy going but he resented his wife's domineering ways and her Baltic high standards of cleanliness and hygiene, which is not a typical trait of the Russian character. Grandmother had intellectual pretensions and she always kept volumes of Goethe and Heine by her bed. I did not come across her a great deal in town and did not take to her much as a child nor later as a boy. I was not very fond of her.

The story goes that Grandmother's brother, a German speaking, provincial Jew from Riga arrived in Moscow and went to visit the Kremlin. Seeing a sentry outside the Palace, he asked in halting Russian, "Which is the Tsar's window?" He was immediately arrested and taken away. When Grandfather arrived at the Police Station, he was told by the officer that his brother-in-law was clearly a terrorist. Hearing this, Grandfather lost his temper and shouted, "Policemen you are? Can you not see that he is a fool? That is all he is, a bloody fool!"

Grandfather was a very generous and upright man with the highest possible reputation in Moscow commercial circles. At one time he owned two textile mills outside Moscow. He also speculated on the Moscow Stock Exchange of which he was a member. After a particularly successful day on the Stock Exchange he would return home with jewellery for my mother and grandmother; sometimes earrings, sometimes a string of pearls. However, his fortunes used to fluctuate a good deal and, in bad times, Grandmother was expected to contribute the bulk of her jewels to replenish the capital. I think she took this quite philosophically. Dowries for six daughters must have diminished Grandfather's wealth but not noticeably. Despite the ups and downs of his Stock Exchange activities, he was still a very rich man at the time of the Revolution. He was quite a gambler and got fun out of it. Nevertheless he was immensely successful and was always the one who had money. After the Revolution, Grandmother buried some of her jewellery in the garden of our dacha but alas could not find it again and we thought someone had removed it. Years later however, when visiting our dacha, I was told that some diamonds had been found in the grounds, and some of the jewellery ended up by means unknown to me, in a bank in Berlin in 1923.

Grandfather was a sturdily built redhead. He had a small, carefully tended beard and was always well dressed. He used to enjoy going to the opera. He liked his food and my earliest recollections of him are of going to his room, either in town or in the country, and being given some exotic fruit to eat. He was most definitely a *barin,* a person of bearing, and well known in the *Slaviansky Bazar* restaurant where he frequently lunched. This restaurant exists to this day and is now the oldest in Moscow having been established in 1873. He was particularly fond of the excellent Russian hors d'oeuvres accompanied by several glasses of vodka. Sometimes he took me with him to choose live fish. Just round the corner in the *Okhotny Ryad,* amongst a collection of small shops and booths selling mostly provisions, there was a splendid shop full of tanks. A long consultation would take place with the shopkeeper before a net was put in one of the tanks and a prize fish extracted, to be delivered to the flat. Grandfather took enjoyment from these things. But in other ways he was quite unworldly. Listening to his daughters talking one day, he asked, "What does the word 'flirting' mean?" He received a prompt reply from my Aunt Sonia, who said, "It is useless explaining it to you if you do not understand it by now."

Grandfather looked on my father, his son-in-law, as the son he never had and was enormously proud of his inventions. Father talked about his ideas to everybody and there was no escaping his explanations. But Grandfather never tired of listening and was fascinated by everything. I used to see Grandfather far more than my parents. Although he was driven to the Stock Exchange each morning, brought back for lunch and then taken off again, he did not stay there very late and liked talking to me. We spent a considerable amount of time together, either in my nursery or in his room and he would tell me about his early life, his experiences in business and his youthful aspirations to become an astronomer. Grandfather's education had been limited to Jewish subjects and had not been continued after his marriage so, of course, he had had no opportunity to pursue his ambition.

It appeared from Grandfather's stories that his family had been prosperous for a long time. But early marriages created curious problems. His aunt was married at thirteen and was given an extremely valuable string of pearls. However, she was still a child and thought that her cat would look nice with the pearls twisted around its neck. The cat evidently had a greater understanding of the value of the gift and rushed out of the window onto the roofs of Vilna. According to Grandfather, most of the Jewish population took to the roofs in an attempt to retrieve the cat and the pearls. At that time of course, Jews had very little opportunity for mountain climbing and probably no head for heights at all. I do not remember what happened to the pearls.

Grandfather told me about an incident at one of his textile mills. I heard the same story years later in England when it was repeated to me as a Jewish joke. However I am assured that it actually happened to my Grandfather for he never told jokes or invented anything. When he arrived for his annual inspection of the mill, the wife of a Jewish employee asked to see him and complained that her husband was never at home. The husband was summoned, told that this was not the way for a married man to behave and was asked what he did on the nights he was not at home. He told Grandfather that he went to learn from a great man, a seer, who had many followers who dined with him every night. When Grandfather asked for proof of his powers, the employee said, "The other night he jumped up, pointed to a corner of the room and shouted, 'In such and such a village in Russian Poland, about two thousand miles away, there is a fire'." So Grandfather enquired, "And was there?" The man answered, "What does it matter? But what wonderful eyesight!"

The grandparents spoke Russian in our presence but they spoke German to each other because it was my grandmother's native tongue. Grandfather did not have a preferred language. He spoke Yiddish, German, Lithuanian and Russian but none of them perfectly. The Stock Exchange was full of jokes based on his mistakes in speaking Russian. There was a member of the Stock Exchange called Kissilyov, who for years was known as Idiot Kissilyov because of Grandfather's mishandling of the Russian verb, "to go". Grandfather was explaining to his bank that certain securities were going to Kissilyov but said "*idiot Kissilyov*" instead of "*idyet Kissilyovy*" and unfortunately for Kissilyov, the name stuck.

The Shabbat family lived in considerable style. My mother was born in a vast flat in *Miasnitskaya*, almost directly opposite the Post Office. In the ballroom hung the largest crystal chandelier ever seen outside the Bolshoi Theatre. My grandparents never again lived anywhere with rooms of sufficient size to take this chandelier and it was still in an enormous crate in the attic of our dacha when we left Russia in 1924. Grandfather kept a pair of matched horses to draw a carriage in summer and a sleigh in winter. The sleigh, which had been specially designed and built for him, was Grandfather's pride and joy. It had ivory rails around the seat and a high quality fur apron which covered the passengers' knees and hooked behind them like a curtain. There is a Russian expression "drunk as a coachman" and one day the inebriated coachman overturned the sleigh, rolling my grandmother and mother out into the snow. So Grandfather had to give up the sleigh but he often spoke fondly of it to me.

Grandfather continued to keep up his Judaism and was involved in building the Moscow synagogue largely financed by Lazar Poliakoff, a cousin of my paternal grandfather. He did not however try to force his religion on his children and, although he did not usually eat ham, he would do so if circumstances required. Occasionally I used to see Grandfather put on an Eastern European skull cap, which had a rim like a chef's hat but no height and intone something from a prayer book. He even attempted to teach me the Hebrew alphabet but I do not think that he had much encouragement from my parents. At Passover, he used to conduct the Seder service which, in 1918, was also attended by Captain Dyakanov and his wife. We had the traditional dinner of "soup with bombs" followed by a meat dish. The "bombs" were a sort of dumpling. A chap once got arrested for sending a telegram saying, "Coming home, make bombs." Grandfather read the service in Hebrew but I imagine that it was an abridged version. We only had one Seder rather than two; it had much novelty value but I cannot see everybody sitting through the two consecutive nights observed by Orthodox Jews. However, even Grandfather's Judaism was considerably diluted from that of his Vilna upbringing. Mother told me how, one winter, her grandfather arrived unexpectedly from Vilna. My grandmother rushed into Mother's nursery carrying the Christmas tree and said to the French governess, "Tell Old Mr Shabbat that it is your tree."

Of all our family, Grandfather felt the effect of the Revolution most. Instead of being a rich man able to distribute presents and go abroad to the usual watering places like Karlsbad and Wiesbaden, he became entirely dependent on my father. He had no business to promote, no shares to speculate in, nothing to keep him amused. He was however a very good tempered and happy man and somehow managed to adjust.

*   *   *

My mother, Flora Shabbat, was her father's youngest daughter and always his favourite although her mother preferred the elder sister Sonia. Flora was a beautiful child with long golden curls and a sweet, unselfish nature. My cousin Genia, who grew up in the same block of flats as Mother, said that people used to refer to her as "the saint in flat number seven." As a teenager, Mother was very innocent, even for those days. Men occasionally tried to "chat her up" in the street and, on one occasion, a man got as far as inviting her to have tea with him in a restaurant. She interpreted this as the man not having enough money to buy himself tea, so she gave him a rouble and said she was sorry he was reduced to such poverty and hoped that this would enable him to satisfy his appetite.

After Mother left school, she took history courses at the university, while her sister Sonia who was thought to be artistically gifted was sent to Munich to study art. After a year or so in Munich, Sonia returned to Moscow and my grandmother and mother set out to meet her. At the station, the coachman shut Mother's hand in the door, crushing her fingers but, not wanting to spoil the joy of the reunion, she managed to conceal the pain from her mother. Apparently, Disraeli once shut his wife's hand in the door of their carriage outside the House of Commons and not wanting to distract Disraeli before he made a speech to the House, she also kept quiet.

Before her marriage, Mother went on a grand tour of Europe. She travelled alone and without a chaperone, an almost unheard of enterprise in those days. It is difficult to imagine how she was allowed to go except to say that she could not be influenced very easily. The only fact that remains in family folklore was that she narrowly missed an earthquake in Italy.

The Poliakoffs

When my father was a small boy, he watched a military parade passing his house with his Poliakoff grandmother. He was amazed at the splendid uniforms but his grandmother was unimpressed. With a Russian gesture of dismissal, she told him, "This is nothing. You should have seen Napoleon's uniform. That was really something!" Born in 1780, she was thirty-two in 1812 when Napoleon marched into Russia. This proud old lady, who lived to be one hundred and five, made sure that Father appreciated the distinction of his rabbinic ancestry.

The family, originally named Poliak, was descended from Hassidic rabbis in White Russia, from or near Mogilev. They had immense influence over quite large territories and were sought out by endless numbers of people to give blessings or advice or even to work miracles. Many Hassidim would travel large distances to visit the rabbi's court. It was not unusual for a prominent rabbi to be visited by several thousand Hassidim on the Sabbath and during the high holidays. The Hassidic rabbis were protected by the state and generally had enormous premises housing their courts, with accommodation for followers and advice seekers. Men, who acted as secretaries, collected contributions and arranged their diaries.

Eventually when their prestige and advantages waned, the family turned to money making. They bought the state monopoly for the supply of spirits in the region. Then, in 1861 the Russian government took over the sale and distribution of liquor and my grandfather and his brother left White Russia to set up as railway contractors in the Ukraine. However the Hassidic background continued to play a part in family history. The Poliakoffs' conviction in their family and personal standing remained unshakeable. My father's inventions, especially the recording of sound on film, were seen as an extension of his ancestors' ability to work miracles. Occasionally he would play a Hassidic tune on the piano which owed a lot to Russian folk music but was played mostly in a minor key.

*   *   *

I never knew my grandfather, Lazar Poliakoff, because he died in the Ukraine when I was only two years old. He and his younger brother settled in Kremenchug, a fairly large town in the "Government" of Poltava. They were next door neighbours and partners in a successful railway contracting business. Their main activity was buying forests, cutting them down and floating the timber down the Dnieper river to their sawmill where they were cut into railway sleepers. Grandfather's brother used to visit us occasionally and I remember him helping me across a small chasm in the road in the country when I was quite small. I remember very little else about him except that he was supposed to be a nice chap. He married twice and his children all settled in Moscow.

Business on the whole bored Lazar. He lived like a country squire and his passion was horses. He had sixty riding and carriage horses in his stables. When I tell people things like that, they think it is absurd. Why should a man need sixty horses? He probably required ten grooms to look after them. But this was typical of Russia, the vastness of the land playing havoc with people's sense of proportion. Grandfather used to take part in trotting races on the frozen rivers and, on one occasion, the sleigh hit a snowdrift, overturned and Grandfather was dragged under the snow for a considerable distance, dislocating his shoulder.

Judging from his photograph, Grandfather was a handsome man. He had six children, four sons and two daughters, of whom my Father was the eldest. With the exception of the youngest daughter, who was hare-lipped, they were all extremely good looking, fair haired, blue eyed and totally unrecognisable as Jews, even by Jews. This, together with Grandfather's unusual interest in horses and shooting, gave rise to a ridiculous legend, spread I believe by a Poliakoff descendant in France. According to this story, the family were originally Cossacks. The head of the family received a letter from the Tsar which he considered to be impolite and wanting to annoy the Tsar as much as possible, caused the tocsin to be sounded and ordered the Cossacks to mount their horses and go with him to the nearest Jewish village to be converted.

Grandfather was a very good shot and taught Father to shoot by using blank cartridges to blow out candles at the end of a very long drawing room. By this time, Grandfather must already have been a widower because I cannot believe that his wife would have welcomed such use of her rooms. In these days of computer controlled simulators, the candle blowing method may not recommend itself. Nevertheless, Father became a splendid shot and always took a keen interest in firearms.

Grandfather spoilt Father in every way and was particularly anxious that his son should eat well. Father was naturally abstemious all his life and too full of ideas, even as a schoolboy, to want to waste time on lengthy meals. So, to encourage his appetite, he was taken by the coachman for a drive every morning before breakfast. But relations between father and son were not always smooth. Father was very keen on going to the local circus and would often attempt the less difficult turns himself. On one occasion, having seen a bare back rider jump through a hoop, he persuaded one of the grooms to make a horse circle the yard while he performed the same feat. The attempt failed and the horse, which was unfortunately Grandfather's favourite, was slightly lamed as a result. Grandfather was enraged. For the first and only time in his life, he slapped his son's face. Father locked himself in his room for three days. Grandfather stood outside the first floor window pleading with him to come out but still Father refused. Finally, he heard a commotion outside and looked out of his window to see Grandfather with four men manoeuvring a grand piano. Grandfather said, "Will you come down for this?" And of course, he did.

Grandfather spoke perfect Russian and was liberal minded. He had intellectual pretensions and used to retire to his study to write books on philosophical subjects but made no attempt to have his work printed and none of his writings survive. Although he was in no way an Orthodox Jew, he had some contact with the synagogue. But he also frequently invited the Russian Orthodox clergyman from a nearby church to play chess with him and discuss philosophy. He allowed ham to be served to his children but would not eat it himself. One day, when Father was eating ham for breakfast and it tasted particularly good, he asked his father what made him stick to this superstition. Why did he not taste it at least? Grandfather replied, "I would only say to myself, what a damned fool you have been, not eating ham all these years, so I'd better not."

Grandfather was one of the leading Jewish citizens in Kremenchug and liked to play Grand Seigneur amongst the Jews. The town was within the Pale of Settlement and had a large community of proletarian Jews. Many of these were very poor and lived in wretched conditions. One of Grandfather's business transactions resulted in a bad debt which was eventually settled by him receiving a quantity of cloth suitable for men's suits for which he had no use whatsoever. Instead of selling it to a cloth merchant, he arranged for the rabbi to send him a large number of poor teenage boys. When these arrived, ten tailors were in attendance to take their measurements and the boys were told to return in a week's time. This time, in addition to the tailors, there were a similar number of barbers who tidied up the boy's heads. Only when they had all had their hair washed and cut, were they fitted out in their new suits. The boys were then inspected by Grandfather who distributed some money amongst them.

*   *   *

The three famous Poliakoff brothers were Grandfather's cousins; Jacob in Taganrog, Samuil in St Petersburg and Lazar in Moscow, who became multi-millionaires and prominent bankers and railway owners. Their daughters married into the various European banking dynasties and into German or French aristocratic houses. According to my papa, his Poliakoff grandmother brought up Lazar's wife in her house in Southern Russia. Before the three brothers became really successful, they offered my grandfather a partnership. Grandfather however considered himself to belong to the senior branch of the Poliakoffs, having Hassidic rabbis as his ancestors, and spurned the offer from the then nobodies. What a grave mistake!

The eldest brother, Jacob, was the least famous of the three. He began his business career as a liquor excise collector and later went on to railroad construction and banking. The second brother, Samuil, was known as "the Railway King of Russia." In addition to laying over 2,500 kilometres of railroads, he invested heavily in Russian oil fields, particularly in the Caucasus. He founded the South Russian Coal Mining Society and several important banks. The youngest brother, Lazar, constructed railroads in partnership with Samuil and was one of the leading bankers in Moscow. He invested large sums on the development of industries in Russia and Persia.

The Poliakoffs were famous all over Russia. This was impressed upon my father when he saw the following sketch at a music hall in Odessa. It began with a well known Russian Jewish joke. A man was sitting on a park bench with a dog barking off stage. Another man, identifiable as a Jew by his bowler hat, ran onto the stage away from the dog. The man on the bench said, "Don't you know that dogs that bark don't bite?"

"I know that," replied the Jew, "But I'm not sure that the dog knows."

Then the Jew, accompanied on the piano, did a skit on Pushkin's famous lullaby of a Cossack woman rocking her baby. The refrain of Pushkin's lullaby is, "Sleep baby, sleep. The time will come when you'll ride away to the wars on a white horse and I will not know whether you are alive or not". The Jew rocked a bundle of cloth and sang, "Sleep baby, sleep. The time will come when you'll be building railways like Shmuelke Poliakoff."

Samuil lived in the finest period house in St Petersburg - No. 4 on the English Quay, later called the Quay of the Red Fleet. It was originally built for a favourite of Peter the Great, Alexander Menshikov. Menshikov was the first Governor-General of St Petersburg and second in importance only to the Tsar. He effectively ruled Russia from this house in the three years between Peter the Great's death and his own exile. From 1732, it was used as a military school and a century later, the Decembrists met in this house on December 13th 1825, the night before they rebelled. They were a group of young aristocrats and officers who wanted either a constitutional monarchy or a republic. Because Alexander I died without a clear heir, the Decembrists encouraged the Guards Regiments in St Petersburg to rebel in favour of Alexander's liberal-minded, elder brother Constantine rather than his younger brother, the new Tsar Nicholas I. However, Constantine had no interest in the throne and the Decembrists failed to enlist popular support. Indeed, the whole situation was so confused that many of the soldiers whom the Decembrists led to the central square to demand "a constitution" thought it was the name of Constantine's wife. The revolt failed; several of the Decembrists were executed and over a hundred were sent to exile in Siberia.

Samuil was the last to inhabit "Menshikov's Palace." Lazar, not to be outdone, bought house No. 12 on the same quay and, for good measure, acquired ten estates in the country, although Jews were not allowed to own land.

All three Poliakoff brothers donated a great deal to universities, schools and other prestigious charitable causes for which they received the decoration of Saint Vladimir, sometimes second and sometimes third class. I have a photograph of Lazar, who was apparently the richest of the three, covered in decorations, Russian and foreign. All Russians belonged to one of fourteen categories starting with the peasant and ending with the royal house. The brothers were elevated to the rank of Secret Councillor, roughly equivalent to Lieutenant General. This meant they were *dvoriani*, gentry. Hence they used to add *de* or *von* to their names when they travelled abroad. This explains a remark made to me in London by the father of one of my fellow college students who came from Odessa and said, "I remember your grandfather, the general, when he lost all his money." I was ignorant, at the time, about the Poliakoffs, so I said that firstly my grandfather was not a general and secondly that he did not lose any money. In retrospect, the student's father must have been referring to my grandfather's cousin, this other Lazar Poliakoff.

Lazar's eldest child, Zinaida, born in 1862, kept a diary from the age of thirteen until her death in Paris in 1952. These diaries, which I have inherited, are a rare document of social history of wealthy Russian Jews. Excerpts were published in the same volume as the Russian edition of my book in 1995. The picture of Lazar's family which emerges is not a happy one, with Zinaida's mother striving for social acceptance, not without success. From the diary, she comes across as an unpleasant character and Zinaida was very much in conflict with her. According to another source, Lazar's wife opened the Winter Ball with the Governor-General of Moscow. Clearly, this was a result of Lazar helping the Governor-General's adjutant with his debts.

As a toddler, I saw Lazar's dacha at Sokolniki, where we had also rented a dacha. Enormous numbers of people were taking tea on the open terrace and the flowers seemed twice as large as those in any other garden. All Russians want to go abroad and the Poliakoff family was forever going to European spas but Zinaida said in her diary what a damn nuisance it was. Eventually she was persuaded to travel with her mama in their own railway carriage which however had to be changed at the border of the Russian Empire. The new carriage was painted bright yellow and created quite a stir when they arrived in Vienna.

The Poliakoff brothers had dealings with the foreign exchange, banking and bullion firm, Samuel Montagu & Co. My father-in-law, Gerald Montagu, remembered Lazar's wife, unaccompanied by Lazar, descending on London with a retinue complete with a chef. At the bank, an office had to be left empty for her to undress partially and take out all the bonds which she had been concealing on her body. Sir Stuart Samuel, head of the Bank, used to lend them his house in Hill Street, off Berkeley Square and I believe that he was less than pleased with the state they left it in when they went. Zinaida met Samuel Montagu, my wife's grandfather, when he visited Russia on behalf of Russian Jews in 1886. He was an MP at the time but not yet titled. In her diary, she remarks that he was "a typical Englishman" which is amusing since he was an Orthodox Jew.

The two younger Poliakoff brothers, Lazar and Samuil, were particularly irked about not being barons. I am reminded of the operetta called "The Gypsy Baron" which Father sometimes hummed and which began, "I am a Gypsy Baron / I have money million." All Jewish bankers in Europe were barons of one kind or another. This was brought home to me when I was shown Lazar's granddaughter's large collection of visiting and condolence cards dating from the mid-nineteenth century; almost every other card was from a baron. Lazar and Samuil Poliakoff were Honorary Consuls, of Persia and Turkey respectively, and Lazar tried to persuade the Russian Court to declare his Persian title to be the equivalent of a barony and thus to give him Russian title to match. But his attempt failed because the Commission which considered his case decided that there were no barons in Persia. The only Jewish baron in Russia was the railway magnate Horace Ginsburg and he was not a Russian baron because his titles came from Hess. When Ginsburg was made a baron, he felt that he could not enjoy his status while his father, Joseph, remained a plain Mr. So he bestirred himself and persuaded Hess or another German principality to make his father a baron as well.

I think the Ginsburgs considered the Poliakoffs rather nouveau riche, although their wealth did not date from the eighteenth century either. Their salon was different from the Poliakoffs', consisting chiefly of artists and intellectuals. From the memoirs and Russian history books of this period, it seems that Baron Horace Ginsburg was a respected figure. I was lent a French biography of him by a distant cousin of my wife, whose husband was half-Ginsburg, half-Sassoon. Baron Ginsburg was an Orthodox Jew and the biography recounts the story of how he refrained from opening a letter from the Tsar which arrived on a Saturday until after the Sabbath had ended. The author thought it splendid that curiosity did not get the better of him.

The author of this French biography disapproved of the Poliakoffs because either Samuil in St Petersburg or all three brothers gave a substantial amount of money to the University of St Petersburg at a time when it was almost impossible for Jewish students to study there. However, some Jews must have been admitted because the donation resulted in the "Poliakoff riots" of St Petersburg recorded in Trotsky's autobiography. Trotsky was, of course, Jewish. The money was intended to fund a new building such as a hall of residence that would have benefited the students, but the students did not want handouts from arch capitalists and there were demonstrations during which Trotsky, then a student, was arrested for the first time.

*   *   *

In 1970 my son Martyn and I took the company car to Russia to an international Exhibition in Sokolniki. We hired a splendid driver from Intourist. Alexander Petrovich was with us for two weeks and took no time off. On the way to the exhibition, he stopped the car and said, "This is a Jewish church. Would you like to have a look?" Visiting Moscow's main synagogue was not on our agenda but he knew we were Jewish and clearly thought that we ought to go. We were greeted by a hefty man who spoke to us in Yiddish which I do not understand. So I replied in Russian. He said, "Russian, better still". He was delighted when he heard our name was "Poliakoff", and told us that Lazar Poliakoff, my grandfather's cousin, had built the synagogue and had been president of the Jewish community for some years. My maternal grandfather, Solomon Shabbat, had apparently also participated in the foundation of the synagogue. In her diary Zinaida records "the solemn opening of the new synagogue." Lazar's father came from Orsha near Mogilev in White Russia to stay with them in Sokolniki for the occasion. The diary records several incidents of her mother not letting the children have the horses to drive out to Moscow. So, anticipating problems with the horses, her grandfather arrived with his own, all the way from Orsha, about 2,000 miles away!

We were taken into a small room at the back of the synagogue where six or eight men were studying. They had beards and burning eyes, like Rembrandt's portrait of the old Jew. The main synagogue was beautifully maintained and there were a large number of women washing the floors. We were shown the commemorative plaque and taken to meet the rabbi whose name was Levin, and who wore a black Homburg hat. He had a small beard and looked almost like an old fashioned academic. This was still the period when Jews were not allowed to emigrate and I was careful not to ask him any awkward questions. Martyn meanwhile was sitting in silence and Levin asked me whether he spoke Russian. I said that he did and added that his mother was from a very old established Jewish family, the Montagus. Without a moment's hesitation Levin said, "Ah, so his grandfather was Shmuel Montagu." I was taken aback, not only by the speed of his response but by the incongruity of hearing Samuel Montagu referred to by the Yiddish version of his name.

One day a man collecting for charity visited Lazar in his house in Moscow. The man had a book with him in which people entered their name and how much they were donating. Lazar quickly saw that no one had given more than 1,000 roubles. So he wrote down 10,000 roubles, closed the book, gave it back to the man and wished him good day. As soon as he had been shown out, the man opened the book, curious to see how much Lazar had pledged. When he saw what was written there, he thought that Lazar had made a mistake and went back and said so. Lazar opened the book, said, "Quite right, how kind of you to point it out," and added an extra nought making it 100,000 roubles. This proved to be very effective as a piece of PR.

Lazar's brother, Samuil, believed he had caused his brother-in-law Varshavsky's suicide by refusing to lend him a million roubles to meet the date on a bill of exchange. He therefore insisted on following the funeral cortege on foot in the depth of a St Petersburg winter and as a result died quite suddenly. There are many other stories about the Poliakoffs, the authenticity of which is seldom provable. According to family tradition, Samuil felt ashamed of his meanness to his brother-in-law and in his will, directed that the heirs were to pay a year's wages to all employees of the Poliakoff railways. The principal heir, his son, was less than enthusiastic about this stipulation and did not pay immediately. However, his hand was forced by a message from the Tsar, to the effect that "gentlemen paid".

Samuil's early death spared him the problems faced by his two brothers. A crisis befell Lazar's enterprises and in 1908 he had to be saved by the State Bank, which effectively put a lien on all of his assets in Russia, including his ten estates and his houses in Moscow and St Petersburg. He was however spared further unpleasantness by the Revolution.

There was very little money left by the time Vladimir, one of Lazar's sons, settled in England, but he nevertheless managed to buy a very large house in Queens Gate Gardens, Kensington. Vladimir had studied railway construction at Moscow's technical university where only one other Jew was admitted in his year. In England however he worked as Assistant Diplomatic Editor of The Times. So he wrote and lectured on politics and also published some historical novels on Russian themes. Vladimir's daughter, Vera, was a great beauty and appeared on the stage for a time, under the name Vera Lindsay. When I made her acquaintance, she was still a very impressive looking woman; tall, majestic and quite formidable. Vera became Lady Barry when she married Gerald Barry, editor of the News Chronicle and subsequently head of the Festival of Britain, for which he was knighted. The family was, of course, Jewish but her funeral was held at the Russian Church in Knightsbridge. I was told that she had made all the arrangements, chosen the music and generally produced the whole event. Her two sons were there; Richard Burton, from her first marriage, is a well known architect and is working on the new British Embassy in Moscow, and her younger son, Stephen Barry. Vladimir is mentioned in several autobiographies of the period and seems to have had an imposing personality. He was quite a difficult man and Mireille, who married Vladimir's grandson Richard Burton, has said that she found him a terrifying figure.

Lazar's son, Alexander, was at the dinner party given by Colonel Gardenin in Zagorsk, while we were staying there just after the October Revolution. Father told me that Gardenin had enjoyed teasing Alexander, insisting on smoking his pipe and then complaining that it was not working very well because it needed cleaning. The stories about Dmitri, Lazar's playboy son, were endless. He had a carriage drawn by four mules and was reputed to have brought back one hundred and sixty five pairs of shoes from Paris as a gift for his mistress. He eventually married and settled in Berlin where his wife opened an haute couture establishment and Dmitri used to buy designs from my cousin Mouma in Paris. My tutor, Nikolai Nikolaievich, also came across Dmitri Poliakoff on his travels and was struck by his restlessness and by the number of times he changed his clothes. There is also a family legend with some circumstantial evidence to support it that Anna Pavlova, the famous ballerina, was Lazar's illegitimate daughter.

The eldest brother, Jacob, built himself a palazzo, known as "villa Poliakoff", in Biarritz. His two daughters, I believe, perished in the Holocaust. I only became aware of their existence when my wife Ina and I called on an elderly French countess who owned a vineyard outside Bandol in Provence. She took us out to lunch and asked about "les demoiselles Poliakoff" from Biarritz. With the possible exception of a family in Italy, I do not believe that there are any Poliakoffs left in the West, including in Russia. It is, of course, an ordinary Russian surname; the head of the Cossacks in Paris was General Poliakoff, and the architect of the Leningradskaya hotel in Moscow was also a Poliakoff – but our family seems to have died out, apart from my children and grandchildren.

Father's Early Years

My father, Joseph Poliakoff, was born in 1873 in Kremenchug, a fair sized town in the Ukraine. He became an inventor in telephony and sound reproduction and, at the end of the last century, was one of the first people to record sound on film. By the end of his life he had something like one hundred patents in his name. His contribution to sound films is recorded in a number of Western books on the history of talking films, and in at least one edition of the Soviet Encyclopaedia.

Entry in the Soviet Encyclopaedia (ca. 1955)
Poliakoff, Joseph Lazarevich (born ca. 1877 — year of death unknown) — Russian engineer, inventor in the area of sound in the cinema and of photo-electronic automation. In 1900, while still a student at the Moscow Technical College, Poliakoff was the first to propose a method for using photocells for photographic reproduction of sound recordings. This invention was patented in Russia (Patent No. 8010, granted in 1903) and in USA (Patent No. 680614). Poliakoff constructed an automated selenium photometer (Patent No. 10116, granted in 1905). This apparatus was based on a differential circuit involving two photocells, which is widely used in contemporary technology.
References:- Tager, P. G "From the history of sound in the Soviet cinema"
   Izvestia Akad. Nauk. USSR Ser. Physics **1949**, vol. 13, No. 6;
   Khramoi, A. V. "The origins of electronic automation"
      Electrichestvo (Electricity) **1951**, No. 11.

[Notice that they got Father's date of birth wrong. He was actually born in 1873 and died in 1959]

Joseph was the eldest of four brothers and was considered by his father to be a genius. He was handsome, athletic and came first in almost everything at school. At his gymnasium the masters conspired with him to help poor maths pupils get through their exams, which were supervised by an official from the Ministry of Education, frequently a retired general in uniform. In one particular exam, it was arranged for Father to ask for water, whereupon the school porter brought him an empty enamelled mug into which he dropped a solution to the most difficult maths problems. Then pupils unable to solve the problems put up their hands for water and received the solutions. Eventually, the old general noticed Father's frequent mugs of water and said, "You over there, why are you drinking so much? What did you eat for breakfast?" My father, who was never lost for words replied, "Herrings, your Excellency."

In the autumn, Russians wore galoshes, which were left under the masters' coats at school. It was not unusual for the galoshes of an unpopular master to be nailed to the floor, so that when he stepped into them and attempted to walk off, he would fall flat on his face. I do not think that Father was a ring-leader in these pranks but he certainly enjoyed recounting them. A more elaborate trick was played by German twins whose father owned a furniture factory. Having suffered too much at the hands of their Geography master, they arranged to teach him a lesson. They removed the loose leather seat from his chair and had a copy made in the factory with a needle soldered onto the springs. Then they changed the seats over and hid the original. The Geography master came in, greeted the form and sat down somewhat heavily on the new seat. Jumping up with a terrible yell, he rushed to fetch the headmaster. Meanwhile the seat was quickly changed. The headmaster came in and began to abuse the form and promise terrible punishments. Then he started to feel the seat carefully with his hands. Finding nothing he gently lowered himself onto it. Still there was no nail. So he said to the master, "Sir, you are mistaken. There is nothing here. It must have been something in your trousers."

Few Jews were allowed to live in the capitals, nor in central Russia and the only Jews allowed to go to university were those pupils of the gymnasium who graduated with a gold medal. These were allowed to study in the capitals and to live there after graduating. In this manner, Father went to the technical university in Moscow known as the Imperial Technical School where he read Physics. In his second year, Father was taken by a friend to visit the Shabbat family. It was impossible for him not be impressed by Grandfather's carriage and pair for Father knew all about horses, and the sleigh for winter was quite magnificent. But he was puzzled by the Shabbat household for, in spite of signs of wealth, there was no manservant and the whole of the large staff was female. This was less strange than he thought because only people brought up with a manservant would generally employ one. My mother was a very good looking but shy girl who still had a French governess and Father did not have a chance to get to know her on his first visit. But they became engaged before Father obtained his first degree. When Father finished at the Imperial Technical School, he went to Germany to arrange his post-graduate work and to rent a modest flat. He then returned to Moscow for the wedding.

In those days, German students spent a good deal of their time fencing and some were heavily scarred all over their faces. Once Father was sitting in a café when a particularly disfigured young man came in and sat down by himself. After a while, he walked up to Father, clicked his heels, bowed and handed him his card. This was clearly meant as a challenge to a duel. Father said that he would meet him by all means but was curious to know why. The young man replied, "You stared at me."

31

"I see," said Father, "Well, I cannot fence but I am quite a good shot and I would be delighted to meet you with pistols." The student, not surprisingly, declined to be shot.

My parents went to live in Germany while my Father worked with Professor Wirtz at the University of Darmstadt. Around this period, my Father produced a number of important inventions, the most notable of which was a mechanism to control the aperture of a camera automatically by means of an exposure meter. The patent is dated 1905. An article in a modern Soviet technical journal described this invention, labelling Father as the father of all automation. The author maintained that this was the first time that the intensity of light had been translated into mechanical action. Father went to New York to try to interest Kodak in his invention. What struck him most about New York was the lack of formality. People in offices, he told us, typically sat with their feet on their desks so that you saw the soles of their shoes as you passed office windows.

At the height of his German phase, Father had a curled up moustache like the Kaiser. In 1913, his moustache no longer curled up but he had more of a moustache than in later years, when his English phase had begun. Father's first visit to England was in 1914 before the First War and he visited again in 1916 and 1923. His admiration for England and all things English became increasingly pronounced and eventually almost everything Father possessed was made in England. This included his sporting guns, fishing rods, clothes, shoes and luggage. He considered, not without reason, English table manners to be mandatory and when I appeared at meals, he enforced them in no uncertain way.

Father's German patent for recording sound on film is dated 1898 but the invention must have come earlier because it takes a while to be granted a patent. The method was substantially the same as it is now; the sound waves were recorded photographically on the film. However its application was very limited because there were no electronic valves and therefore no amplifiers. Without amplification, you could only just hear the soundtrack through a pair of headphones, so the invention had no future in cinemas until valves appeared. Even then, the original sound films used gramophone recordings, which were more or less synchronized with the film, so that when the actor opened his mouth some sound came forth.

When my parents returned to Moscow, they acquired the flat in Manege Square. When the flat was to be furnished, my Father's habitual insistence on top quality and his lack of sense of proportion were clearly demonstrated. In Darmstadt there was a furniture maker to the German Court. After a close study of available designs, Father ordered furniture to be made for the study, the dining room and their bedroom. The furniture, which included a thirty-foot long bookcase, arrived in its own freight car, complete with three

German craftsmen to assemble and install it. The style of the study and dining room was eighteenth century English, while the bedroom was art nouveau. The quality of workmanship was higher than on any furniture I have ever seen, including pieces made in the eighteenth century. The drawers fitted so well that they moved with the perfect smoothness of syringes.

The study was very large and impressive and not nearly as cluttered as the dining room. The furniture was inspired by Queen Anne, modest and in good taste, without too much carving on the chairs. On the left, as you came in, was the enormous bookcase with twisted columns in the middle and an electrically-lit imitation fire. When we moved to the country after the Revolution, it was quite impossible to accommodate the whole of the bookcase in the dacha, and we had to leave two thirds of it behind. To the right was the library table and a leather sofa which went along the wall and around the corner. There my parents' feeling for period went wrong for the corner was surmounted by a vitrine attached to the settee which contained a small collection of English silver toys, mostly little replica Chippendale chairs and some cups of Napoleon's period. My father's very large desk stood by the window with two eighteenth century English, leather wing-chairs. There was a pale oriental carpet and a large, dark bronze chandelier. My papa's Steinway grand piano was also in the study.

Father's friend, Colonel Gardenin, advised my parents on the décor in the small English sitting room. There was a Chippendale library table, an English Regency chandelier in black and gold, very pretty Chippendale chairs and what might have been an eighteenth century settee. As well as having a cultivated taste in furniture, Gardenin had a good knowledge of porcelain marks. This enabled him to make a joke of rather doubtful taste after a dinner party. One of the most famous porcelain factories in Russia was founded in the eighteenth century by an Englishman called Gardner. On one occasion, Gardenin was placed at dinner next to a Miss Gardner. His hostess asked him as he was leaving whether he had enjoyed talking to Miss Gardner. "Yes," he replied, "But I found the experience rather disturbing, for all the time, I wanted to turn her over to see the mark."

Gardenin's brother-in-law was the Italian Marquis de Pasana, who featured in an investigation into American arms dealers because he was an agent of the Electric Boat Company that made submarines in America and sold them to the Russian government. He was described in the newspapers as behaving like royalty. I did not meet him until he visited us in England because he lived in St Petersburg but he was very friendly with my parents who used to dine with him before the Revolution. De Pasana lived on a considerable scale, in a large villa, with a butler and at least one footman. Once, he led my parents into the dining room where the dinner was all set out, looked up and said, "There's not enough light in here, we'll go out." That impressed my papa tremendously. De Pasana left the servants, the dinner, everything and they went to some restaurant. I met de Pasana in Golders Green of all places when we were living in a rented house in Park Drive. He came either to dinner or for drinks and I was deeply impressed by him. The moment he entered the room you became aware of his presence. He was tall with an elegant black beard and he emanated a wonderful warmth together with an almost royal dignity.

My father founded the Telephone Construction Company in Moscow with capital provided by his father-in-law. Father was essentially a sound-reproduction specialist and the company was formed to exploit his inventions in the field of telephony. The quality of sound on telephone networks was sadly neglected at that time and no one worried as long as they could more or less make out what the other person was saying. In particular, telephones suffered a great deal from interference on the lines and reducing this was one of Father's principal patents. The Telephone Construction Company did not make the main telephone exchanges but offered a superior alternative. Father won business by demonstrating his system over a reasonable distance and comparing it with the customer's existing equipment. He was full of the times when the men from Siemens or Erickson, the manufacturers of the main telephone exchanges, had to use his system to give instructions to their men at the other end. But to get orders for complete telephone installations, the exchange and all the subsidiary equipment, it was necessary to make friends with different heads of administration. This of course meant entertaining and drinking with them. Father could not keep up with the Russian drinking so his friend Gardenin became his "drinking director" and drank with the customers.

The company had quite smart, well maintained premises in the centre of Moscow. Sometime early in the First World War, the company acquired a substantial engineering works which machined castings for various purposes and made specialised military equipment. The English Marconi Company had a share in both enterprises and a number of well known figures including the merchant banker, Riabushinsky, became shareholders.

Before the Revolution, Russia was being industrialised very rapidly and, in certain areas, compared favourably with the West. The best textile mills in the Russian Empire were well ahead of the Lancashire mills, although all the equipment was English. The Posnanskis in Lodz had the largest textile mill in the world with fifty thousand employees. Despite being Jews themselves, they would not employ Jews, because they thought they were troublemakers. My mama was at a watering-place without my papa, when Madame Posnanski arrived with a suite including her own chef and various secretaries. She ignored my mama completely until my papa arrived and was paged by men going round, shouting out that Krupps, the top German engineering firm, wanted to speak to him on the telephone. Father had recently invented a cable in which the inner tube expanded as much as the outer tube so that there were no breaks. This was before the coaxial cable was introduced and Krupps were considering his patent. Of course, Madame Posnanski heard the message and after that, she invited my mama to tea but Mother would not go.

Father was a pioneer of motoring in Russia, and bought an Adler in 1909, the year before I was born and while my parents were still living in Germany. It arrived with two bodies. In the winter it was a landaulet, like the old London taxis and in the summer, it became an open car. The car would be sent to the works for the bodies to be changed and a crane would lift the unwanted body off and replace it with the other. It was upholstered in grey and had a partition and occasional seats. A silver vase in the centre of the partition always carried two or three carnations. The windows could not be wound down but were controlled by a belt punched with holes, like in the old railway carriages. You pulled the belt up or down and fixed it at whatever hole you thought would suit your requirements. With his usual thoroughness, Father went to the Adler factory to be taught maintenance as well as driving. He was never able to find an entirely satisfactory driver as most of them were coachmen with very limited experience of cars. Rather than drive Mother somewhere, they would claim that the car would not start. They could not be left to do any maintenance by themselves and I remember sitting in the driver's seat of the open car while Father and the driver were de-carbonising the engine. About a year after the Revolution, the Adler was requisitioned when the Telephone Construction Company was nationalised. Thereafter the car functioned from the works and when we left Russia it was still running with a pick-up body having replaced the other two.

The first manservant employed by my parents arrived from his village in shoes made of birch bark. He had never been in town and training him was quite a thing. My papa began by rigging him out in livery not unlike a butler's and took him to a shoe shop where he bought him two pairs of shoes. The shoes were wrapped up and Father asked for them to be delivered. But his manservant said, "I know these people. We'll never see them again" and insisted on carrying them home under his arm. Father had a whole series of stories about his behaviour before he was properly trained. I still remember one of them. When the telephone rang, he used to summon my papa by shouting, "At once! To the telephone!" I do not suppose that my father ran.

After the Revolution

Soon after our return from Zagorsk, Father decided that it was no longer safe for us to remain in Moscow and that we should go abroad through southern Russia. Our bags were packed and everything was made ready for our departure. But when Father told the senior people in his company that he intended to leave, a deputation of managers and older workmen arrived and pleaded with him to stay. I had not been aware either of our imminent departure nor of the preparations being made and I never saw the work people so I suppose they came to the offices not to the flat. Emotions must have run high at that meeting. Father came home. All he said was, "Unpack" and we remained in Russia for another seven and a half years.

Against tremendous odds, Father managed to keep the Telephone Construction Company going for another year and it was one of the last private enterprises to be taken over by the state. When the banks were closed very soon after the Revolution, there was no means of paying the work people. Father called a meeting at the works. He stood on a box and addressed several hundred people. "Any one of you can chuck a brick at me standing here," he began, "But that will not feed your families." He said that he could not pay them because his account at the bank had been blocked and he invited a deputation to accompany him to the newly formed Ministry of Finance. The Commissar of Finance must have been rather shaken when a dozen or so rough looking men in workmen's winter clothing burst into his office accompanied by my papa. Father's clothes made no concession to the Revolution, so the Commissar immediately pointed to him and said, "You speak for them". Father argued his case and the bank account was unblocked.

Almost all city families went to live in the country from May to late September. Even the lower middle classes had access to dachas and others went to the villages they came from. Most men however travelled to town every day. I was born in 1910, at the end of August by the modern calendar and on 7th August by the old one, in a dacha in Lasinastrovsky between Mamontovka and Moscow. A few years later we rented a dacha at Perlovka and I have a photograph of Mouma and me feeding chickens there. Then Father was abroad and we rented a small dacha in Mamontovka which was on the Northern Railway between Moscow and Zagorsk. That summer, Grandfather displayed interest in another dacha, also in Mamontovka, which he eventually bought. There was a long period of negotiation. Every day he would meet the owner, agree a price then the following day the owner would ask for more.

Our move to the country heralded a much freer lifestyle than I was accustomed to in town. To begin with, I was put off by the absence of town noise and passing trains would wake me. But, by the end of the summer, I would be used to silence, and would hardly register the steam engines hooting now and again. Conversely, the town noise would disturb me, but it did not take me long to adjust. There was always a certain sadness when the summer came to an end but town held its own delights and the first snow was a great thing.

Quite atypically, when I was in the country at the age of three or four, I had a fight with the cook's son and I was reprimanded by my parents. My governess came across me sitting on the pot with tears trickling down my face. "Don't cry," she said, "Nothing terrible has happened." I replied, "You do not understand. I have no free will over crying or not crying. When something bad happens, funny things go into the eye and produce tears. It has nothing to do with me."

That was considered a remarkable explanation from such a toddler. I do not remember the fight at all, only looking through a window and seeing the cook punishing her son with a carpet beater, and then my sitting on the pot and offering the "scientific" explanation as to why people cried.

Every year, Grandfather used to set out to hire a dacha for the coming season, which had to be very large because, in addition to our usual household, my aunt Sonia and cousin Mouma often joined us bringing their own staff. The dachas were unfurnished so like most people we kept a complete set of furniture in store. This would be delivered to the dacha, a few servants would go ahead to set it out, and then we would arrive. However, after Grandfather bought the dacha in Mamontovka, our "summer furniture" was permanently installed. Our dacha was larger than average. As well as the main house, which was two storey, it had substantial outbuildings including a two-roomed gardener's cottage, a Russian bath house for the servants and a small cow shed.

We were in the country in the spring of 1918, when the authorities decided to requisition our Moscow flat. Perhaps its proximity to the Trinity Gate caused them to fear assassination attempts on the Party leaders or perhaps they needed an impressive place for Kalinin, the President of the Republic, to receive people outside the Kremlin which was now heavily guarded. Most ministers had flats inside the Kremlin but Kaminev, who married Trotsky's sister and was one of the original Bolsheviks, was given a flat in our block in Manege Square. It may even have been our flat. We were given a week to vacate and were surprisingly allowed to remove not only all the furniture but also the silk from the walls of the study. We took as much furniture as could fit in the dacha and the rest was put into store. The Moscow staff: Adam our manservant, Luba our cook and Polya our parlour maid were all transferred to the country and from then on we lived in the dacha all year round. Fortunately, the ground floor could be adapted for winter use as there were Dutch stoves and double windows throughout. The first floor however had no heating or insulation and could not be used in winter.

The first winter at the dacha was quite different from anything I had experienced before. Our only neighbours were a prosperous middle-aged business man called Sarafanov and his nephew Ivan Ivanovitch. They lived by themselves with only Sarafanov's old nurse to look after them. We visited each other after the evening meal; they would come to us one night and we would go to them the next. We drank weak tea; Father played gypsy songs on the piano and Sarafanov attempted a little singing. Ivan Ivanovitch talked to me about his hobby, breeding fish. Sarafanov's old nurse used to hover in the background giving advice on how to cure ailments, like a sty in the eye, by uttering ancient prayers and burning strange herbs. Outside there was deep snow with only the sound of an occasional train hooting as it passed the station. All the other dachas were empty and the nearest human habitation was the village of Listviani about one and a half miles away. Sometimes, we were visited by peasants from this village. As many as twelve at a time came to drink tea. When they had had enough they would turn their tumbler on its side which meant, "I've had enough but, if you insist, I'll have some more." Eventually they would turn their glass upside down, a sign that no amount of asking would be of any use.

Ivan Ivanovitch was in his late twenties or early thirties. He had no job and spent quite a lot of time with me, particularly in winter. That first winter he taught me to ski, mainly cross-country, but there were some hills on which to show off. We had more than one pair of skis because the skis had to be wider and longer for deep snow. Before I went to school, I virtually lived on skis in winter. I went with Ivan Ivanovitch on quite lengthy trips into the forest and I skied on our own land, over even quite short distances because there was no other way of getting about.

Our almost complete isolation during the first winter at the dacha was broken in the second by the arrival of my Shabbat grandparents from Moscow. They had stayed in the interim with my mother's sister, Aunt Sonia, either in her flat in Vasdvizhenka from which she was thrown out in due course, or in a temporary flat. When Vitia, Aunt Sonia's husband, left Russia, she and her daughter Mouma also moved in with us. This resulted in serious overcrowding when the top storey could not be used in winter. In summer, I had a room of my own but in winter I found myself sharing it with my grandparents. My grandparents had lived with us for as long as I could remember but there was a difference between that and having them in my bedroom. Yet I do not remember feeling any kind of resentment. I think that children accept that kind of situation without any revolt. My parents had a room with an en-suite bathroom. Polya, our maid, and Luba, the cook, slept in the maids' room. The only rooms without beds were the dining room, which contained Father's Steinway grand piano and the kitchen. The silk with the fleur-de-lys, taken from the walls of the study in Moscow, adorned the dining room walls as well as those of the much smaller study where Mouma and her mother slept. In winter, our manservant Adam was much better off than the rest of us with his two rooms in the gardener's cottage.

Despite the crowding we got on very well. In summer, we used to eat breakfast and lunch on the east facing terrace, which was fairly large and roofed over. We ate dinner on the west facing terrace which was glazed and had a spectacular view as the ground dropped to a stream and one could see the village in the distance. Neither terrace could be used in winter. The dacha also had two quite large balconies on the first floor (in Russia called the second floor) which were again for summer use only.

I spent most of my time with Mouma who was only three months younger than me. In spite of the three beds in my room, there was still space for a small billiard table, a table for our lessons and a very smart school desk for me. Mouma invariably beat me at billiards and very frequently at croquet but was not much use at chess. We played cards, principally with Grandfather: a game called "Preference", a type of three-handed elementary bridge and a game I have never come across anywhere else called "Six and Sixty". Mouma was much better at arts and crafts than I was and used to make useful containers out of birch bark. As nothing could be bought at this time, and certainly not in the country, presents to our elders and to each other had to be drawings or poems. I wrote one for Sonia's birthday and remember the last line which read, "I hope you will eat many birthday cakes without fearing the Bolshevik."

I had received no instruction of any kind during the first winter at the dacha. Jeanne, my much loved Swiss governess, had been repatriated and Father was away until late at night. Mother also spent much time in Moscow with her parents and sister. At this stage, I was able to read and write as easily in French as in Russian but knew very little else and, feeling the need for regular study, I took matters into my own hands. I found a Russian book on the subject of breeding dogs in Father's bookcase. It was largely concerned with mating and I could not understand most of the advice but felt it was valuable knowledge and memorised it page after page. When Mouma arrived however, our education could no longer be postponed. Maria Pavlovna, the headmistress of the village school situated two miles away, was persuaded to come every morning to give us lessons in Russian, History and Arithmetic. She taught us until lunchtime and then we were expected to do a certain amount of homework, in particular to write essays. Mouma did not find this easy and there were many troubled scenes when Sonia pleaded with me to tell Mouma that I too found essay writing difficult, but I absolutely refused. I did not find essay writing difficult and the fact that I was better at something than Mouma pleased me, for this was not often the case.

Maria Pavlovna was a sturdily built woman, slightly larger than her husband. Her teaching was adequate but uninspired. We did not feel any great affection for her but got on quite well with her children, a boy and girl, and spent a good deal of time with them, particularly in the summer. Together, we invented a secret language, and composed a dictionary for it. For some time we produced a newspaper partly in our language complete with illustrations. Maria's husband was joint head at the village school but was fairly ineffectual and there was another woman teacher who was quite pretty and had a husband who worked in Moscow. The two families lived above the school sharing three rooms between them. Our visits to the school building were quite rare but we did go to see a play directed by Maria's husband. We travelled there in a peasant's sleigh and the peasant allowed me to drive on the way there which proved to be a much greater thrill than the play itself. The play was concerned with the liberation of the serfs and was acted by young men and women who were ex-pupils of the school. Maria Pavlovna's husband came on stage to introduce the play but made rather a poor showing. The audience laughed and made remarks such as, "What is the matter with him? Why is he picking his nose?" At the end of the performance, the cast stood stock still singing, "Freedom, Freedom, Freedom, Freedom." In the summer, Maria Pavlovna's teaching was supplemented by an eccentric French woman who insisted on climbing through our gates instead of opening them. She used to come a few days a week to teach us French. My Swiss governess, Jeanne, had spoken French to me all the time so I was completely bilingual as far as conversational French was concerned, but my knowledge of academic French was slight.

Our lives used to change abruptly in May when all the "summer only" dachas filled up. Many friends and relations came to live in dachas within walking distance of ours and life for the women and children became almost a continuous party. Meanwhile the unfortunate husbands continued to work in town, leaving by train early in the morning and returning in time for dinner at night. The women and children visited each other for tea or, more rarely during the hungry years, for lunch. My aunt, in particular, was extremely sociable and needed more external stimulation than my mother. She used to take Mouma, who was likewise more outgoing than me, across the tracks to visit the smaller dachas. Aunt Sonia, or Tante Sophie as I called her, was quite a cultured woman and had very good taste in music, literature and the decorative arts. She had quite a circle of artistic friends who appeared from time to time at the dacha. I remember one man, a painter or art enthusiast, pointing out the colour of the sky, discussing what should be done to reproduce it and generally trying to interest Mouma and me in painting, although of course there were no galleries in the country.

For the children, life centred around the tennis courts. There were four red courts adjacent to a football pitch and a large gravelled space with benches where people gathered in the evening. The tennis courts were near enough to the dacha for Mouma and me to be summoned to lunch by means of a cow horn. Children were allowed to use the courts until midday; the afternoons and evenings were reserved for adults. Our game improved steadily and by the age of twelve I played better tennis than I ever managed to do in England. We used rather tired pre-Revolutionary balls which bounced very little making the game quite fast and when new Slazenger balls became available from England, our game was upset for a couple of weeks.

I do not remember ever feeling bored or wanting to go back to the city. On the other side of the football pitch, less than five minutes walk from our dacha, was unspoilt forest. It was quite large and I never reached the other end of it. In the autumn it was a splendid place to collect mushrooms which is a very important Russian sport. I spent much more time outdoors than Mouma and in the summer months used to go for long runs with Ivan Ivanovitch. He was a most interesting companion for a boy of eight because he knew all about animal, insect and fish life, trees and natural history. Ivan Ivanovitch was an established expert on fish breeding and helped me with my aquarium, which was quite large and elaborate. We collected most of the plants from the stream at the bottom of our land. I had fancy fish – some very small ones, some bigger and tropical creatures that looked like lizards. In addition to these which my papa bought in town, we had dug in our stream (which belonged to us but was outside the perimeter of our grounds) and found all sorts of beetles which we put in the aquarium. To clean the aquarium we had quite a few snails that stuck to the glass and seemed to enjoy eating the yellow deposit on it.

One of the summer visitors was a Russian Jew with the Tartar surname of Yacoob. He and his family used to stay in a dacha about a hundred yards from ours. Yacoob and his wife had a reputation for always quarrelling. They had two children, a girl and a boy who was very cheeky. One of the first things he asked me was, "How much does your father earn?" I was deeply shocked, firstly that he should ask such a question and secondly that I was expected to know. But I remember Yacoob chiefly for his tale of how he was with a friend, one autumn when it was raining and misty and they felt terribly sad. They had to do something to shake themselves out of this misery so they decided to break one of the headlights of a passing locomotive. This required a certain amount of courage. They found a long stick and, standing with one foot over the rail, Yacoob waited for a train to appear. He held the stick lightly; at the moment of impact, he stepped back and the train passed with the driver swearing at him like the devil. Now that was an extraordinary thing to do but the sense of having achieved something, lightened their spirits. It was not immediately obvious what the achievement was, but his account of it was a work of art.

Our forest was beautiful in winter. The tall pines, firs and occasional birch trees were thickly covered in snow. Tracks of hares and other creatures could be seen clearly and there was an extraordinary stillness all around. Where Sarafanov's land finished, there was a road which descended very steeply towards the village, made a sharp turn and then went up equally steeply. This was my favourite hill for skiing. It was very fast because the ice became compressed where the peasants' sleighs passed and there were snow drifts on either side. Once I fell when I was moving so fast that I went completely under the snow head and all. It took me some time to learn to ski down that hill without falling. Then Ivan Ivanovitch encouraged me to try without sticks which was the ultimate test. I was not allowed to go to this hill alone because the bend might have concealed a peasant sleigh coming in the opposite direction but surprisingly, Mother seemed quite willing to accompany me and stand at the bottom of the hill where she could see both ways and tell me when the coast was clear. On one occasion, we arrived to find a group of boys on skis attempting the hill. We were greeted with derision, "Here comes the little master with his mamma." The boys were my age or older and not peasant children but from a colony. Peasant children would have been at school and any way would not have had skis. They used to go about in a horse and sleigh and did not walk around or do any physical exercise for pleasure. Colonies were homes for orphans and street children. This must have been a superior colony, almost a boarding school, or they would not have had skis. The children were not clad in uniform free issue clothing but nor did they wear fur coats like me. Mother, clad in her sealskin coat, went down to her usual post at the bottom and I waited. Three of the boys went down the hill and each one fell although they were using sticks. I waited for a peasant and his sleigh to pass, then I threw my sticks away ostentatiously and went down the hill, without falling, to the general acclaim.

Our diet deteriorated steadily. My papa was abstemious and did not worry unduly about not getting much to eat but the servants were concerned. I used to chase round the kitchen garden, picking out peas that were ripe, or nearly ripe, and in season we had strawberries and other soft fruit. For breakfast Mouma and I used to have porridge. Certainly there were no more caviar breakfasts! It soon became very difficult to obtain white flour. We bartered little bits of silver and valuables with the peasants for flour but the bread made from this tasted pretty awful. Mouma's doctor, who used to come from town to see her, decided that she needed a special diet and should have white bread. Although I was not a particularly pleasant child at that time, I put up with seeing Mouma have delicious bits of white bread to munch, while I had to lunch off what looked like a mixture of badly milled rye and sawdust.

Relations between my mother and grandmother were not of the best and I felt very defensive of my mother. My grandmother was not mistress of the house in the country anymore than she had been in town but she could not help interfering. On one occasion, Grandmother and Tante Sophie were laying into Mother, asking, "Do you have to give so much to guests? There is so little to eat. It makes no sense." Mother was obviously suffering, so I yelled out, picked up a plate and threw it at the two of them. The plate missed but succeeded in silencing them. We Poliakoffs have a temper which can only be roused by our own family. It can be dangerous but is very useful for keeping discipline. Very many years later, I was having lunch with Mouma's daughter, Betka and her husband in a small restaurant in Paris when I said, "Well, all Poliakoffs have this temper." Betka's husband replied, "Yes Betka has it too. I said something to her and the next thing I knew, there was a fork stuck in my stomach and four little holes."

For a time, the peasants accepted pre-Revolutionary money for food and my Mother had wisely drawn a large sum from the banks before they closed. In the first six months, we were not hungry. Even when the money was finished, we could barter with peasants, exchanging silverware, clothes and household utensils. Our silver samovar kept us going for some time. But soon the peasants around Moscow had nothing to spare and the family went through a very hungry period when a typical dinner consisted of a small portion of boiled millet, or some other *kasha*, with a few drops of sunflower oil. In retrospect, the situation was rather amusing for, apart from the food, nothing else changed. It was still served by Adam on old Copenhagen china, the table properly laid and the silver polished although how well was difficult to judge at night since there was no electricity. Once when I had to answer a telephone call to wish someone happy birthday, I returned to find that my plate had disappeared and that my dinner had been finished in the kitchen. There was nothing else to eat, not even any bread, and I burst into tears.

When the last grains of millet had been eaten, Father would tell us about his day, making even minor incidents seem lively and exciting. The family would forget their hunger and the servants, having cleared the table, would stand by the stove, listening. One night he told us how he had rescued the three Gireau brothers from internment. The Gireaus were the Courtaulds of Russia. They came originally from Lyon and had become the largest silk manufacturers of the Russian Empire. At least one brother was a shareholder in Father's company and Father was determined to get them released. So he went to their main factory and called a meeting. Addressing the assembled workforce, he commented on their good working conditions and reminded them that these were due to the benevolence of the proprietors. He asked the workers whether they realised that the Gireau brothers were interned, quite unjustly, in a monastery. Then he said that he manufactured shells for the Red Army (which of course was untrue) and that he needed the Gireaus to work in his enterprise. This persuaded them; Father collected a deputation and off they went to plead for the three brothers. The commissar responsible for their internment said, "Fine, you want them to work in your enterprise; I will release them during normal working hours but then they must return to the monastery." This day-release scheme went on for a considerable time until the brothers were eventually repatriated to France. One brother was desperate to visit his mistress, who lived in the country, near a station on the Northern Railway. It was clearly a very dangerous enterprise and there had to be a fool-proof excuse. So the man was provided with a letter, which said that he was being sent to test the telephone lines at the appropriate station, he was given some kind of measuring instrument and off he went to his mistress.

Father travelled to Moscow every day for he was still running the Telephone Construction Company and he came home just in time for dinner. All the carriages on the Northern Line were open like modern carriages, not divided into compartments. As a result, conversation was not limited to people sitting next to each other but could easily become general. People used to admire Papa's clothes or the propelling pencil he had purchased in London. I was present on at least one occasion when Father held a seminar on life in England with people asking questions and expressing doubt about whether things really could be so. My son Stephen's play "Breaking the Silence" fictionalises this period and includes a remark made by my father to a man sitting opposite him on a train going to Moscow. Whereas the majority of *ci-devant* people tried to disguise themselves in rough sheepskin coats and workmen's caps, Father never made any concession to the Revolution. He was always dressed in his splendid fur coat and Savile Row suits and looked the part of a typical pre-Revolutionary grandee. After eying Father for a few minutes, the man said to him, "Comrade, are you not afraid to be dressed up to the nines like this?" Father, who never used the word comrade, replied, "No, I thought that the Revolution occurred so that you could be dressed like me, not I like you."

Father's physical courage was considerable but he also had a temper which, when roused, made him quite dangerous. I was in my parents' bedroom one night during the hungry years when Adam, who was being given some instructions, answered Father back. Blood rushed to Father's head and he shouted, "Because there has been a Revolution, you think you can behave how you like. But I will show you." He ran across the room and tore down one of his shotguns while Adam wisely hurried out of the room. Father went on raging but quietened down fairly quickly. Eventually there was a knock on the door and Adam came into the room holding his high

Persian lamb hat in his hand. He bent low, Russian fashion, and repeated three times, "Humbly I beg your pardon". Father was touched. He threw his arms round Adam and they kissed; both had tears in their eyes. None of this surprised me in the least. If Adam had stayed in the room, Father would have been quite capable of discharging the gun, and Adam knew it. Yet despite being authoritarian, Father was an extremely good employer. He took complete responsibility for anyone who worked for him, whether in his house or in his company. He sent some people to the Crimea because they had lung trouble and helped others with their marital problems and children's education. Years later in England, most of the employees in his company really loved him, although he was quite capable of making scenes and was not infrequently unreasonable.

When the Telephone Construction Company was finally nationalised, Father was offered a senior position in the company but he refused and it became urgent for him to find an official post. Fortunately, a Polish friend of his was the Director of the Northern Railway. This man had been interviewed by Trotsky who asked him, "Are you going to work with us?"
Father's friend answered, "I consider it my duty to tell you that I am a Monarchist."

"I don't care what you are," Trotsky replied, "So long as you work properly".

So, through this friend, Father was appointed Inspector of Telephones of the Northern Railway. This provided badly needed rations of inferior bread and potatoes as well as free passes on the Northern Railway for us all. For good measure, Adam was also enrolled as a railway employee.

It was still impossible to buy clothes and the rations were not enough to feed the seven family members and three servants living in the dacha. On two occasions, to obtain more food, my father undertook inspection trips of a thousand miles or more to the North where one could still barter salt, which was obtainable, for flour and butter. For these trips he was given his own official railway car which was extremely well equipped and divided into a dining room, study and bedroom. The railway provided a man to make tea, cook and clean but Father took Adam with him as well. I do not think that he did anything else for his job as Inspector of Telephones of the Northern Railway except to go on these journeys. He would be gone a week or ten days and presumably he called at the main stations to check their telephone installations but I do not know. I remember being terribly thrilled on going to meet him at the station. His railway carriage arrived with its own locomotive and out came Adam holding a female piglet under his arm. We christened her Margot and she produced endless progeny. In addition to the piglet, they brought a sack of flour, twenty pounds of butter and a little honey. I am sure that winning the pools could not have had a greater tonic effect on the family than this small supply of food.

Better times

Our dacha was larger than almost all of the other dachas in Mamontovka and was visible for miles. So whenever I was asked by village boys where I lived, I had only to point to the one house visible on the horizon. There were a large number of dachas on both sides of the railway track. On our side of the track and immediately opposite us stretched the enormous house known as "Mamontov's dacha". It was situated to the east, between our dacha and the station, and it had some woodland but no view. "Mamontov's dacha" was occupied by a man named Kalmikov, a senior manager of some technical state enterprise, but it had been built by Mamontov, who constructed the railway and after whom the village of Mamontovka had been named. His dacha was wooden, painted white and stretched a very considerable length. Kalmikov once showed Father and me round the main house. It had over forty rooms, each one panelled in a different, fairly rare Russian wood. There were numerous outbuildings including a children's theatre and a dower house. The house was perched just above the station and one could see the flowers in the garden from the platform. The whole site was very narrow. As a result the gates and the drive were peculiarly positioned and I never saw them used. It seems extraordinary that such a vast house should have been built so close to the railway but I suppose it gave Mamontov special satisfaction to hear the trains on the railway he had built.

Immediately on the other side of the station was quite a large dacha which belonged to people called Michelson. They were textile manufacturers. Years later, my late wife and I were in Capri, having lunch *al fresco*, and at the next table there was an early middle-aged woman with a girl. We started talking and it appeared that she was the wife of Michelson of the dacha. When I first mentioned that I was Russian, she said, "You needn't have told me this; the ease you have in talking to people immediately reveals that you are of Russian birth."

Our dacha was identical to Sarafanov's dacha next door which had a larger plot than ours and included substantial woodland as well as a tennis court. The two dachas shared their outbuildings which were semi-detached. From our kitchen you came through to the servants' small roofed terrace, down the steps into the yard. There was a continuous building stretching the whole length of the yard beginning with Adam's two rooms, Dutch stoves, a hall, and then to the right, a Russian steam bath used by all the servants. The building continued with the cellar which was a wooden structure going deep into the ground. In the spring, it was packed to ground level with ice and snow which gradually melted. Food was placed on top of the ice and, as the level dropped, you had to go down a ladder on the cellar wall, to fetch whatever you wanted. Next to the cellar was the servants' lavatory. To reach it, the servants had to go into the yard, through snow in winter, but they never used our lavatory. At the end of this continuous building was a pigsty and there was a cow shed near the gates on the other side of the yard, far from the dacha.

Our dacha sheltered us for seven years after the Revolution. When Father and I left Russia in 1924, my grandfather, who was very ill in bed, said that he wanted to bless me. I knelt down, which was wrong because Jews do not do that but he did not seem to mind. He put his hand on my head and uttered some Hebrew words. Then he said, "You lived in paradise here. I hope you will find something similar again."

*   *   *

To reach the village of Listviani, you walked down the very steep hill where I skied in winter, then made an equally steep climb and Listviani lay straight ahead through fields full of cornflowers and poppies among the rye. When you arrived at the village, you could still see our dacha, white in the distance. Neither Mamontov's nor Sarafanov's dacha could be seen from a distance because both were obscured by trees.

Between the village and our dacha were some other dachas about a mile away in the dip. Mouma and I had friends in one of these and one summer we erected a flag staff and practised signalling messages from one dacha to the other. Listviani was not particularly interesting to me and I seldom went there. The village consisted of a straight road with huts on either side, a two-storey brick built school and a church. It was surrounded by fields for, as in Spain and Italy, the land which the peasants cultivated was some distance from their huts.

The peasants of Listviani were enterprising and prosperous. In addition to farming, they built wooden dachas which they rented to summer visitors from Moscow, and the women and children made containers out of birch bark in which they gathered all kinds of mushrooms and berries to sell. I cannot imagine them not having money. They were like the French farmers in Brittany where Mouma later lived. Mouma and Tante Sophie used to say, "Our farmers are not bourgeois, they are peasants." The tenant of the farm adjacent to their property in France was about to have his land sold from under him. So Mouma's father-in-law offered to lend him the money to buy it. The farmer said he would think about it and then, from under his floorboards, came gold coins and he bought the farm.

Most families had a cow so they had ample milk and made a cheese like *creme fraiche*. But they kept virtually no other animals and I do not know whether they ate very much meat. Their diet consisted largely of milk, bread and boiled vegetables and their basic food was a soup made with cabbage called *shchi* in which occasionally there might be bits of meat floating around. On holidays, they would perhaps eat a large cockerel or goose. The German manufacturers of chamber pots suddenly found that they were selling millions of pots to Russia. They could not understand why there was such a huge market. So they went to find out. They discovered that they were not being used as chamber pots but by peasants to put their soup in. The soup was set in the middle of the table and everyone dipped their spoon into the same pot. The chamber pots, as the peasants discovered, lasted for life and were undoubtedly cheaper than regular saucepans.

The male peasants wore coloured Russian shirts buttoned on the side, dark trousers and long boots. In winter everyone had *valinki*, felt boots, because if you walked through the snow in ordinary boots you would freeze. Superior *valinki*, like mine, were trimmed with leather which looked very smart but otherwise *valinki* were not particularly attractive. On holidays, the peasants used to drink like anything and, as far as I could tell, their other principal entertainment was for the head of the family and the headmen of the village to visit us. I think the young ones quite enjoyed themselves. They used to gather in the evenings and flirt. They had a very healthy life. We had the best possible relations with our peasants and I never met a dissatisfied person among them.

Peasant children, both boys and girls, went to school so they could read and write and knew enough arithmetic not to be cheated in markets. But a good proportion of the older peasants were illiterate. This did not prevent their conversation being of interest because they formed their own opinions, rather than taking them ready-made from the newspapers. They spoke mainly about the pre-Revolutionary years. Egor, the butcher, once told me how he had found his bride. One day, when he went to market with his father in the horse and cart, he was left holding the horse. Opposite was a splendid young woman also holding her father's horse. Egor badly wanted to talk to her but did not know how to start. Then a young man went up to her and started a conversation. "So," he said, "I saw what to do. I rushed at him, knocked out a few teeth and threw him to the ground." Naturally she became his wife.

The only peasant hut I remember visiting was Egor's. He was very tall and had a vast number of children. There were no shops, so after he had slaughtered an animal, he would sell the meat himself. He was a rich peasant and had a small beard. You could tell a great deal about people from their beards. Most peasants had unkempt beards that were never trimmed and grew as long as they would go. Some provincial Jews may have had similar beards and sages or famous rabbis had sensational beards that grew to a considerable length. Coachmen had beards but neater and smaller than peasant beards and

· Adam, our manservant, was clean shaven. Otherwise there was the very carefully trimmed Edward VII type beard, known in Russia as a *Poincaré* after the French president, which was sported amongst others by the President of the Republic, my maternal grandfather, Colonel Gardenin and my doctor, Shapiro. On the whole, however, the people who came to see us were clean shaven. So Egor's small beard signified that he was more urbanized than the other peasants.

The interior of Egor's hut consisted of the usual largish room, which occupied most of the hut, in which there was a table and benches. The main feature of the room was the stove, quite large and standing proud of the wall, on top of which the oldest member of the family, the grandfather or grandmother would be sleeping. This gave rise to the familiar exchange,

"And your grandfather, is he still alive?"

"Oh yes. He's over there, he's sleeping on the stove."

But what was unusual about Egor's hut was the little partitioned area with a bed, where Egor and his wife slept, while all the children slept on the benches around the walls in the main room. This was unusual luxury; normally, the whole peasant family slept in one space with no partitions. They built their huts themselves and had no lavatories or baths. The peasants were self-ruled. They divided the land as required and all their cattle grazed together. When a peasant married, everyone helped to build him a hut and he was given land. When one of Egor's sons got married they knocked down all the partitions in the hut for the wedding and it had to be reconstructed afterwards. I did not go to the wedding but my parents were guests and Adam was best man. The bridegroom, I was told, wore tails and white tie.

*   *   *

Every summer there was an attempt to turn us out of our dacha by various organisations which wanted to build a home for orphans, a rest house for workers or tubercular patients, or just a nice place for a commissar to go to in the summer. All such attempts were successfully fought off by Father. But possibilities of disaster were never far away. One year, a committee was set up in the village with the power to impose a once and for all tax on "former people". The chairman and secretary of this committee duly arrived at our dacha demanding 50,000 roubles from Sarafanov and Father. Neither had anything approaching this sum and the discussion appeared to be getting nowhere when Sarafanov suddenly said to the chairman, "I have some photographs I'd like to show you in the other room", and told the secretary to stay and talk to Father. Sarafanov then handed the chairman 2,000 roubles and said, "You keep this for yourself, and Poliakoff and I will each pay 5,000 roubles tax". The chairman was delighted and suggested that this would be an appropriate time to open a bottle of vodka.

Arbitrary taxation paled into insignificance next to the appearance of brigands in the countryside following the Revolution. Presumably these were deserters from various army units or dispossessed people who had managed to get hold of guns. I was very frightened by stories of brigands torturing people while looking for hidden money or valuables, but some of the brigands were quite gentlemanly. A neighbour of ours, while walking through the area of woodland that led to the station, was held up by a man with a revolver. The man told our neighbour to hand over his wallet, which he promptly did. The man then asked the price of a return ticket to Moscow, took just enough money out of the wallet for the ticket, a tram fare in town and the price of a modest lunch, and returned the wallet.

Just down the road from us (turning right at our gates) lived the Yokishes. They were Russified Poles and lived in the only dacha built of stone because they had suffered badly from fires. Mrs Yokish used to come to tea and entertain mother with horror stories of brigands. One story was of a woman who told a brigand that money was hidden in the cellar. The brigand went to the cellar taking the woman's son with him as a hostage but she locked him in the cellar nevertheless. The brigand then cut off the child's ears and threatened to kill him if the woman did not let him out.

Like many people, Mrs Yokish buried jewellery in her grounds. My grandmother buried hers in broad daylight. Mrs Yokish must have done so within the sight of her cook who removed the jewels and pretended they had been stolen by an outsider. The police arrived with dogs who sniffed round the hole and then went straight to the cook. She was heavily interrogated. You could not expect Russian policemen at any time to be particularly correct and they probably beat her up. Eventually, she confessed and said that her husband, a locomotive driver on the Northern Railway, had hidden the jewels in a cylinder normally used for oil. The police went to find the husband and probably beat him up as well, although they already knew on which engine the jewels were concealed. The Yokishes received all their jewels back still somewhat covered in oil. This incident caused a sensation in the district and of course Mrs Yokish told the story in the greatest possible detail, no doubt embroidering it freely as she went along.

Father was a great believer in acquiring the best equipment for whatever he did. He had a collection of shotguns, pistols, fishing rods, cameras and tools of every kind which he kept in perfect condition and he developed considerable skill in using them. His interest in firearms became very useful during the troubled times after the Revolution and, in spite of searches, Father never surrendered his weapons. Two shotguns loaded with dumdum hung on the wall in my parents' bedroom, and Father slept with two Brownings and a silver plated Belgian revolver by his bed. That I think shows a certain lack of a sense of proportion because after all, he only had two hands. In the country, it was unthinkable to go out at night without a gun. To get to the station, you had to pass through a little copse and, when my parents went out in the evening, my papa would put his hand in his pocket, release the safety catch on his gun and hold the gun by his side until they emerged.

From time to time the telephone would ring and a neighbour would appeal for help because he was being besieged by brigands. Often the neighbour would actually be shooting it out but was worried that his ammunition would not last much longer. Father would telephone Adam and a few neighbours. Armed with shotguns and revolvers, they would collect at our house and race through the snow to help the besieged neighbour. These sorties were terrifying for us, for we could hear shots without knowing what was happening. My grandparents were invariably upset and would try to dissuade Father from going out. Mother never said anything. I was frightened out of my wits for Father, but also did not say so. Usually they would all return about half an hour later, in the best of spirits to have tea, very pleased with themselves, and having seen blood on the snow, they would assume that they had scored some hits.

The atmosphere of shooting it out persisted for quite some time and, after a while, I thought it the most natural thing in the world to handle firearms and to expect to use them. One night, when the servants had left to meet Father at the station and I was alone in the dacha with my grandparents, the dogs set up a terrible howling. I assumed that someone was in the yard and felt that I had to do my bit. So at the age of nine, I took down the loaded shotgun from the wall and issued out on to the servants' balcony to protect the homestead. I remember that I was not frightened of someone shooting at me but of the recoil of the gun giving me a nasty shock. I could not see anyone to fire at in the pitch dark, so I retreated. However, the howling increased and I rushed out again and stuck the barrel of the gun into Father's stomach just as he was coming up the steps. The safety catch was off and he was not in the least bit amused. I do not remember being complimented on my bravery.

*   *   *

A stranger called one summer and asked to use the telephone, having seen a telephone line going to our dacha. In fact, we had two telephone lines. The Northern Railway provided a service telephone, which was installed in Father's bedroom while the ordinary telephone was in the hall. The service telephone stood on a colossal desk, surrounded by a series of measuring instruments and resistance boxes that Father had managed to salvage from his laboratory in town. All this was purely for show to impress people wanting to requisition our dacha. The man used the telephone in the hall but the door to the bedroom was open and he could see the apparatus. He asked what it was all for so Father told him about the Telephone Construction Company and the Northern Railway. The man then introduced himself as Schmidt, Commissar of Labour. He said that his department was moving into to a new building to be called the Palace of Labour and that he had been trying to build a new telephone exchange without success because there were no switchboards or other equipment to be had. Father thought that there must be some stocks about and said that he could easily organise it for him. The Commissar asked Father what made him think he could manage it when he himself had failed. Father answered, "To the people who matter in the telephone world, you are here today and gone tomorrow - but I will always be a Poliakoff." Within a week Father was installed as Communications Manager of the Ministry of Labour. He received the contract for the exchange and completed it in good time.

As a government official, Father was entitled to special rations of food. The first ration he received was a large quantity of salt herrings. We had a wonderful dinner; herrings for hors d'oeuvre, followed by herring soup and then herring fish cakes. Our enjoyment however was short lived for it was summer and the herrings had to be put into the cellar. The cellar was at the very end of the yard and during the night, all the herrings disappeared. I think Father let it pass. There was now quite enough to eat and pears, oranges, tangerines, French wines and brandy - luxuries unheard of for many years - started appearing on our table.

The Commissar was extremely impressed with Father and made him head of a conglomerate called Standard Trust, which included a construction company and a number of other activities. He was entitled to the use of a car, and a horse and sleigh in winter. This was helpful as Father's own car had been requisitioned but the cars from the conglomerate's garage were all pre-war and on their last legs.

Father's status rose steadily and a continuous procession of peasants passed through the house who wanted jobs, or help with their grazing rights, or whose relatives had been locked up by the government. Though paying lip service to the new regime, the peasants remained much as before; religious and very much aware of the need to respect people with influence. Father was unquestionably regarded as the leading citizen for miles around and he was able to help them both materially and with advice. On one occasion, a deputation from the village called at our dacha. The men sat about, drank tea and appeared to have difficulty in making their request. Finally their chairman spoke. "We know you are not of the same religion as us," he said, "but the roof of the village church is leaking and we have to raise the money to repair it." Father, who was relieved that it was only a question of money, naturally gave them more than they asked for.

Our dacha originally had no electric light and oil lamps and candles provided only modest illumination. Father was determined to have electricity in the dining room at least and achieved this with the help of the Station Master of Pushkino, who delivered six enormous accumulators which were placed under the piano. A lampshade with a rather feeble electric bulb was installed over the table and connected to the accumulators. Every few weeks or so the accumulators were changed for newly charged ones. The Station Master thus became a frequent visitor to the dacha and on one occasion followed Father about all the evening, repeating in a plaintive voice, "Please lend me money to buy a cow" until in the end Father gave in.

Some of Father's prestige rubbed off on Mouma and me. We all had free passes because of his involvement with the railway and, after a little while, I did not even show my pass but used to go though the control saying, "Communications Service". Later, when I went to school in Moscow and wanted to telephone the country, I did not have to tell the operator our number but simply picked up the receiver and said, "Northern Station please." When the Northern Station answered I said, "Poliakoff. I want to speak to my house" and I would be put through. But this privileged treatment did not go to my head and I never told the people at my school of the advantages I enjoyed.

*   *   *

In the summer of 1922, when I was twelve, Lenin introduced the New Economic Policy, universally known as NEP. This allowed some free enterprise and partially restored the capitalist market economy. New businessmen, known as "nepmen", made money quickly and the black market flourished. But NEP did not affect my family a great deal. My papa was an inventor not a businessman and, although Grandfather had previously speculated on the Stock Exchange, his wealth was solidly based on his cloth mills. We came from a totally different milieu; buying a large piece of leather, waiting for the price to go up and then selling it was not the sort of activity in which my family ever engaged.

NEP did however completely alter the atmosphere in Mamontovka. There were more summer visitors than ever, with money to spend, and the entrepreneurial drive spread to the peasants who began to charge more for their dachas. The nepmen felt suitably disinclined to walk the mile or more from the station to their dachas so the peasants polished their *proletka*s (small open carriages identical to the horse cabs in Moscow) and dressed their sons as coachmen to meet the tired husbands who commuted to town. All sorts of French wines appeared and I tasted my first claret which, however, was not particularly distinguished. Occasionally there were brass bands, concerts and musicals on the newly refurbished small stage in the recreation grounds and the tennis courts were in constant use. Even a restaurant was opened for the first time in Listviani. I never saw the restaurant myself but we were told about it by the chairman of the village who called on us fairly regularly.

In this optimistic atmosphere, our neighbour Sarafanov bought himself an imported motorcycle with a side car. He could not manipulate the machine himself and had a driver to take him to town and back daily. Sarafanov was obviously a fairly rich man and also the sort of chap to benefit from NEP. He had quite a grand establishment in town which I never saw but my parents visited for dinner or for a party. He was quite handsome, athletically built and aged about forty-five. He had no wife but he made up for it by taking an interest in somebody else's and the servants talked about their liaison quite a bit. She looked very Russian and was almost a beauty but she was a little plump, and had a very nasty small boy.

Sarafanov had to have everything of the best and my papa bought his old motor boat when he replaced it with the latest model. For a long time the motor boat languished in a shed by the river but the day arrived when Father decided it was safe to take it out of hiding. He brought two drivers from town, who managed to get the motor going after several years of disuse, and we started out on our maiden voyage: Father and I, the two drivers and their wives who had dressed for the outing in white dresses and coloured ribbons. But to my bitter disappointment, the motor gave out after less than half a mile and would not start again. The scenery, at least, was rewarding. The river Ucha was not tremendously wide but flowed between banks which gradually got higher and higher as we drifted downstream. There was a pretty display of water lilies and further along one could see at a distance a high colonnaded house which had once belonged to the wealthy Morozov family.

All this relaxation however was premature. The authorities were provoked by reports of a former capitalist being driven around in a motorcycle and side car, and Sarafanov was tipped off that there were moves afoot to requisition his house. So Sarafanov and his nephew, Ivan Ivanovitch, dug an enormous hole in the nearby forest, packed up the motorcycle and side car in waterproof sheeting and buried it during the night. This did not, however, prevent their dacha being requisitioned to house a high-ranking official called Sasnovski and his family. Sarafanov did not move very far away. He had money and bought himself another dacha. I do not remember visiting him there but I think Father used to meet him on the train going into town. Sasnovski did not move in immediately and for a few weeks, his brother was installed in the requisitioned dacha. There was great indignation when this happened because the brother, far from being a junior minister, was a nepman. A well known Soviet poet called Demian Bedny, or Demian the Poor, lived in Mamontovka and Sasnovski appeared to be a friend of his. Soon after Sarafanov's house was requisitioned, Father met the poet on the train. Demian asked Father, "How do you like your new neighbours?" "I don't know," Father replied, "But tell me, where is Communism in all this?"

Demian, who was a Party member, was not amused.

A few days after Sarafanov's dacha was requisitioned, I woke up in the morning unable to shake off a terrible dream. People were again trying to evict us from our dacha and this time they were succeeding. The dream upset me profoundly but I did not tell anyone about it, since attempts to turn us out were fairly frequent and were always successfully fought off by Father. We ate breakfast as usual on the east terrace and had barely finished when about twelve men, a couple of women and two senior policemen descended on us. They had a signed order to requisition our house and all its contents. They took a very long time going round the house, making an inventory of everything and they found our motor boat and requisitioned it on the spot. We were a household of twelve, including my grandparents, aunt, cousin and four servants. We stood to lose all we possessed and where were we to go? Meanwhile, another party descended on Kalmikov who occupied the vast Mamontov's dacha opposite ours. The shock to everyone was very great indeed because although large scale requisitioning had been frequent in the early years after the Revolution, it was now thought to have come to an end.

Father rushed to town to see Schmidt, the Commissar of Labour. "If this is done to me," he said, "I will want to leave the country immediately with all my family. If I am not allowed to do so, I will shoot my whole family and myself since we have nowhere to go, and make quite sure beforehand that everyone knows why I did it." Schmidt was suitably impressed and went immediately to the ministry which was going to evict us. "I don't care what happens to your other requisitions," he told them, "But Poliakoff's must be stopped at once." "At once" translated into about a week, after which we received an order exempting us from the requisition but instructing us to house everyone turned out of Kalmikov's dacha. Kalmikov was a gentleman and told Father that he did not intend to inflict his family upon us but that his relative, who had lived in the dower house, fully intended to move in. Fortunately, Father managed to buy a small vacant dacha for him and so we were saved.

*   *   *

Lenin's New Economic Policy had no immediate effect on our diet but our food situation improved dramatically when Father developed the grounds of our dacha into a farm. First came a cow called Malishka and needless to say, I was at the gate for the welcoming ceremony. The peasant selling the cow had tears in his eyes and the cow appeared equally upset. Malishka was made to step over a rope stretched across the gate and was offered a piece of black bread covered in salt which she licked. The rope was an indication to the cow of a change of ownership and bread and salt are the usual Russian welcome.

The existing cow shed was quite small and, when calves were born, more accommodation was needed. Father drew up plans for a larger shed designed to keep the cows warm in winter and had it built under his supervision. Over the cow shed was the hay loft where my fancy pigeons were kept and I could let them out by pulling on a string to open the hatch. They were tumbling pigeons that turned over backwards in flight. Father had given them to me as a present and I kept them, at least in principle, although the clearing out was done by Adam. On one occasion I was watching their aerobatics when two buzzards tried to get at them and chased them round and round. I rushed to Father to ask him to shoot down the buzzards. But he would never shoot a gun before checking that there was no obstruction in it and, by the time he was ready, the buzzards and pigeons had all gone. Fortunately, however, the pigeons returned that evening.

The farm gave us a great deal of interest for it seemed as though one of the animals was always giving birth and new life appeared at every season. We ended up with pigs, sheep, ducks, five cows, several beehives, one hundred chickens and some geese. We ploughed up the ground between our fruit trees to grow potatoes as well as most other vegetables, particularly red and white cabbage, which was salted in barrels for the winter. Vegetable marrows and pumpkins grew to an enormous size. The farm and the house were protected against brigands by a security system far in advance of the times. Burglar alarms were fitted to the cow shed and the house was guarded by dogs on chains attached to an overhead arrangement that looked like the power supply to trams and enabled them to patrol a considerable area without being able to escape. All the servants were from peasant families and knew how to milk cows, slaughter chickens and so on. We managed everything ourselves except for ploughing which was done by a peasant. And we encountered few problems, although we had some ducks which started dying for no apparent reason.

I was not expected to help with running the farm but occasionally I took the pig to nibble the grass outside the house and I enjoyed lifting the potatoes and discovering the extent of our crop. A single seed potato could yield up to ten potatoes but the average yield on our ground was probably about seven. I also cultivated a small plot on which I grew pumpkins and vegetable marrows. I looked after the chickens, not in the sense of clearing out the chicken run but by collecting the eggs and keeping the books. I knew all the chickens by name and I used to write down how many eggs each had laid. So, over a period, one could read against a chicken's name whether it had laid a hundred eggs or forty-five. This had unfortunate consequences because if we were thinning out, the chicken who had laid only forty-five eggs would be eaten. Then, there was the task of discouraging chickens from brooding which I considered a very useful activity. This involved catching a chicken that had spread its feathers in preparation for sitting on eggs, and pouring water over it which it did not enjoy at all. Once I drove the cows to the village, from where they were taken to graze with the peasants' cows. It was quite a long walk for our cows and usually they were escorted by Adam or a maid. I was teased by the village boys who knew at once who was a *barchuk*, a little master, no matter what one was wearing. I had made myself a long whip with a crack louder than a pistol shot and knew how to make just the right movement of the wrist to get the required crack. This was very effective both for letting the cows know that I meant business and for keeping the village boys at a distance, for it could give quite an unpleasant cut.

We became completely self-supporting with the exception of flour which came from the peasants, probably in exchange for piglets or chickens. We even made our own cherry brandy, which was not terribly strong but much praised. We had much more milk than we needed, even after making butter and cream cheese and I suppose the rest was given away to neighbours. Occasionally there was a state levy on milk producers who had to deliver milk to the nearest collection point, which for us was at the next station north, called Pushkino. On one occasion, I went by train with Ivan Ivanovitch to deliver our quota. We carried the milk in two open pails for we had no other containers. The pails were quite heavy and in fact I think Ivan Ivanovitch carried both. A very officious woman, wielding a float gravity-measure, accepted them with a compliment, since our milk was neither skimmed nor watered. The unfortunate man in front of us in the queue had his milk rejected with a tirade against the wreckers and swindlers still to be found in our communist country. When I went to school in Moscow at the age of twelve, there was a medical inspection at the school and one test involved blowing into a tube and seeing how far the cylinder went up. I have always been very thin and my blowing was not very good. The cylinder did not rise much and the woman doctor was very worried about me. She said, "Are you sure you are adequately fed?"

So I said, "Yes."

Then she asked, "Do you get enough milk?"

That was too much for me and I said, "We have five cows!"

Malishka, our original cow, calved one winter but, after a few hours, grew feverish and seemed to be dying. The news spread to the village and an audience of peasants arrived and sat around in the cow shed shaking their heads. The local butcher Egor was there with his implements, wanting to slaughter the cow before it died so that he could sell the meat. I had, by invitation, watched Egor slaughter a cow before. He would stun the animal by hitting her hard with the blunt edge of an axe between the horns. The cow would fall down, he would slit her throat and collect the blood as it ran out.

Father arrived from town and absolutely refused to have the cow slaughtered. He consulted his veterinary text book and discovered that the right treatment was to pump oxygen into her udder. Of course there was no oxygen and the nearest vet would have been miles away but Father reasoned that air would do just as well. He got hold of a large hypodermic needle, disinfected a bicycle pump with a bit of rubber tubing attached to it and, with Adam's help, blew up the cow's udders and tied the teats with the little pink and blue ribbons usually used in Mouma's hair. All this took place in front of the peasants and the butcher who made remarks such as, "All towns people are mad. Does he think he is pumping up a tyre?"

When the operation was finished, Father went to wash his hands in the house. About half an hour later, he was getting ready to have dinner when Adam rushed into the dacha in a state of great excitement. The cow which had been lying on her side reconciled to death had struggled to her knees. An hour later she got up and started chewing the cud. The peasants were amazed and declared it a miracle. The village talked about it for a week. The left wing said, "Our cows die like this, but they live for the bloody capitalists." Mother said that she was far more proud of Father having saved the cow's life than of all his inventions put together.

*   *   *

Our five dogs were very important to us, particularly in the early days, both as companions and for peace of mind. With the dacha, we inherited a collie called Toosik who was used as a guard dog in the yard. Toosik had a charming personality. He was very affectionate and in no time became a member of the family. He was however accident prone. When let off his chain, he used to stroll down to the station to look at the trains. As a result of excessive curiosity, he was run over by a train but fortunately, it only cut off a bit of his ear. On another occasion he managed to get stolen. My father was ill in bed at the time and we feared that he had caught typhoid on a train. So we were plunged in gloom. But a few days later I was sitting in my father's bedroom talking to him when the door burst open and, to our great joy, Toosik bounded in and jumped on Father's bed. There was a piece of rope around his throat which he had obviously chewed through.

Then there was Major, a Doberman Pincher. Major was a very clever dog who supplemented his diet by stealing eggs, both from us and from the neighbours. He would listen for the clucking of a hen who had just laid an egg, jump over the fence and take his prize. He did not eat the egg at once but carried it back to his kennel to savour at his leisure. If intercepted on his way, he would relinquish the egg without excessive protest. He was not chained and his escapades all over the district earned him one death threat too many. Clearly, he had to be found a good home in town where there were no eggs to steal. A couple of years later, when Father was driving in Moscow, he happened to see Major wandering into a courtyard. Stopping the car, he rushed to follow him. Major turned, saw Father, almost knocked him over by jumping on him and lovingly licked his face all over.

As the farm expanded and there were more animals to steal, we acquired two more guard dogs. As with Toosik, their chains ran on a contraption that enabled the guard dogs to cover the whole area of the yard. Tom, the Chow, was an extremely fierce dog who did more menacing, growling and barking than any other. Peasants used to come to the dacha carrying on their head a substantial cage of large chickens or plants for the garden or flowers or fruit to sell. We would look at their wares and perhaps buy something but you had to watch these entrepreneurs because, if you left them alone, they would promptly eat half the cherries you had just bought. Peasant women also used to come, dressed in long skirts, coloured blouses and head scarves. They sold curd cheese, butter or some other cottage industry product and the dogs had to be held, growling like mad. On one occasion, Tom's chain broke and he rushed at the peasant women whereupon they threw themselves on their knees and started crossing themselves. Tom sniffed at them, almost shrugged his shoulders, and walked off.

I was quite frightened of Tom. My few attempts to pat him on the head were not well received but then one day the poor chap managed to get his paw frozen, probably from having licked it in very severe weather. He was feeling very sorry for himself and I thought I had to do something. So I took off my gloves and held his paw to warm it up. He seemed intensely grateful and never snapped at me again.

But my greatest friend was Zaliva, my father's harrier who looked like a foxhound but was larger and black and brown. Like Major, the Doberman Pincher, Zaliva virtually became my dog and considered herself as such. Every now and then she had puppies. She would disappear for a few days and then come out to find me and guide me through the labyrinth under the house to view the newly born. On one occasion Father went shooting with a few friends and took Zaliva with him. They travelled some considerable distance north by train. When a harrier scents a hare it starts barking, the pitch getting higher and higher as it gets closer. During the chase nothing else existed for Zaliva and when she was in this state, someone in the forest was able to steal her. Father returned without her. I could hear him groaning in his bedroom while I was crying my eyes out. The loss of Zaliva was unthinkable so Adam was sent down to the station where they had disembarked, saw the station master and told him that when we found whoever had stolen Zaliva, my papa would arrive and shoot him. This had the desired effect and the dog was released. Since she was very intelligent, she remembered that she had come by train and went to the station and presented herself to the station master. The station master then telephoned us and Adam went to fetch Zaliva to the tremendous relief of us all.

*　　*　　*

I often went to the station on summer evenings to meet the train on which Father returned from Moscow. One evening he got off the train carrying a long brown paper parcel. He would not tell me what it was but said that it was a present for me now that I was almost twelve. The walk from the station to the dacha, took only about seven minutes but it seemed to take much longer on that occasion. When at last we reached home, Father said, "I thought that it was time you learned to shoot" and he unwrapped the parcel. It was a single-loading rifle, the sort used to shoot down things at fairs. To my eye, it was a thing of great beauty. Two nails were fixed above my bed on which the gun could hang but, unlike Father's two guns, it was not loaded. That evening I was allowed a few practice shots which I did not find too difficult.

There was a local association through which people registered their sporting guns with the police and were helped to obtain the appropriate cartridges. The secretary of the association had the same surname as us and often came to fill our cartridges with powder and shot. Soon after Father had given me my gun, the secretary summoned all the local shotgun owners to a small celebration where I, and for good measure Mouma, were to be initiated into the fraternity.

About thirty people arrived and sat around in front of the dacha. The peasants had no culture of having guns and using them against hares or vermin. The only exception was the Cossacks who were expected to arrive on horseback with a rifle when summoned. So the people attending my initiation ceremony were probably middle class people who rented dachas in the summer and came by train in the winter to shoot. By that time there were also many people who like us lived the whole year round in the country.

I knelt on one knee in front of the secretary who touched me with my gun and proclaimed me a member of the hunting fraternity of our district. The same was done to Mouma and then somebody counted, "One, two three, shoot", and we all discharged our guns. I do not know what our neighbours thought about this but I imagine that by that time they were not afraid of another Revolution.

My parents with Sonia (Mouma's mother, right foreground) and my Grandparents Shabbat. The picture is thought to have been taken shortly after my parents' engagement.

The dacha in Lasinastrovsky where I was born. Dated 1st September 1910.

Father during his German phase.

Father during his English phase, London 1914.

My Mother

*With Mouma and Grandmother
Shabbat, a picture from
Mouma's album.*

*With my nanny.
Dated 6 May 1912.*

With my cousin Mouma in 1914.

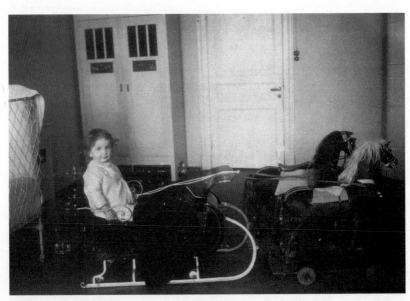

In my nursery with my favourite toy, a scale model of the Moscow cab sleigh.

The farmyard and animals at Mamontovka, as painted by Mouma.
The Chow Tom (1) used to frighten me; Malishka (2) the cow which Father
saved with a bicycle pump; the Russian cow (3) with Beauty (5) and Mary
(6); Toosik (4) who was stolen and came back; Major (7), the Doberman
Pincher, who stole eggs; Margot (8), the piglet from the Northern Railway
who, in turn, produced many piglets of her own.

My parents, photographed shortly before they married.

Festivities

My papa refused to make any concessions to the Revolution and my birthday continued to be celebrated every year on an unprecedented scale, as though it were the combination of an important national holiday and a flower carnival. Tremendous preparations went on. The entire fence surrounding the dacha was decorated with garlands made of pine branches from the nearby forest, culminating in triumphal arches on the east and west entrances. In spite of the shortage of supplies, a large scale baking operation took place and something like sixty guests were entertained for the whole day. Most of the guests came from town, others from neighbouring dachas which were inhabited only in summer.

Father composed the music and supervised the costumes for elaborate charades that he thought out and rehearsed with Mouma and me playing the leading roles. One year the charade was on the name Poliakoff. There was some kind of ballet for *pol* meaning floor in Russian and a ladder was brought in for Yakov, signifying Jacob's ladder. Then, I jumped up and of course lots of people guessed it. Another year it was chess which in Russian is *shachmati*. *Shach* means sheikh so I sat wearing a turban while Mouma danced round me to Arabian music and *mati* was Mother. I am afraid that birthdays became something of a strain for me, what with the acting and so many guests.

Preparations for one particular birthday were slightly disrupted because of an assassination attempt on Lenin in Moscow in August 1918. A young Jewish woman named Fanny Kaplan had succeeded in wounding him and this resulted in extensive searches and arrests. Father gave his shotguns, three revolvers and a chest of our best silver to Adam and told him to hide them without telling us where they were. The dacha was wooden but built on brick foundations and, underneath, there was a labyrinth of passages between brick piers through which one could crawl with some inconvenience. Adam dug a grave in the least accessible part of this maze and hid the guns and silver there. About twenty soldiers arrived and sentries were posted by the "triumphal arches" and elsewhere while a search party looked for weapons. While they were still in the house but had finished searching my room, someone rushed in to hide a 6 lb bag of sugar under my bed. There was such a scarcity of sugar that there was a good chance that the soldiers would have helped themselves. The soldiers found nothing but they were amazed by the garlands and the preparations and kept asking what they were for. They were astonished to discover that the cause of all this fuss was a small boy's birthday. Soon after the search, the guns were dug up because they were needed for protection against brigands, but the silver was left where it was.

As things stabilised, more people came to see us, particularly for festivals. During Shrove Week, a large party would sit round the dining room table. Three or four servants carried in pancakes, one at a time, in closed pans. When they pressed a lever on the handle, the pans opened and a very hot pancake would fall onto the guest's plate. The guest would then help himself to melted butter and caviar which he would spread liberally onto the pancake. The average consumption was something like twenty pancakes per head and that was just the hors d'oeuvres. This is not quite as shocking as it sounds because Russian pancakes are very thin. Decanters of vodka stood all along the table and there was the usual Russian business of toasts. Like Father, my mother had no interest in food or drink but, even in the hungry years when the next day we would be eating boiled millet, she had the typical Russian attitude to feeding guests. The meal, needless to say would last for hours and, at the end, Father would go to the piano and play popular gypsy folk songs. Those who could sing did. Most were not shy and especially not after such a lunch. Towards the evening, two or three peasant sleighs would arrive for the traditional joy ride. The younger people and children would bundle into the sleighs and be driven about for an hour or two. Whenever a sleigh came to a hill, one or two guests would be pushed out of the sleigh and rolled down it. All this was expected during Shrove Week.

The main preparation for Easter, as far as I was concerned, was to help colour eggs and decorate them with transfers which were wetted and stuck onto the fragile shells. We produced quite a large number of eggs and exchanged them with the servants and anybody who came along. Transfers were not available after the Revolution but we went on colouring the eggs and my cousin Mouma, who was artistically gifted, created some original designs. Then there was the *pascha*, a cheesecake made with eggs, sugar and butter in a pyramid shape with crosses and flowers from a mould, and *kulich* which was a tall, undecorated cake made with lots of eggs. Before we ate them, the servants took these cakes to the midnight mass at the church to be blessed. Of course, Easter marked the end of Lent and these cakes were made with all the foods not eaten by Orthodox Christians during the fast. I think that we exchanged presents and were visited by the usual guests. Russians say, "Christ has risen" and reply, "Indeed he has." Then they kiss three times on the cheek. As far as I remember, when the peasants came to congratulate us on the holiday, they were kissed also. But not by me; I was small, the peasants were large, they had terrifying beards and I do not think the operation appealed to me in any way.

*　　*　　*

When we lived in the country after the Revolution, Christmas began with a peasant arriving in a sleigh. In modern terms, the peasant sleigh corresponded to an estate car. It had no seats as such, only straw at the bottom and you sat where you could. We drove to the forest and Father would look at trees. The forest was magical; silence, thick snow, the occasional animal passing - perhaps a hare in its white winter coat and bright sunshine. My papa would choose a tall, handsome fir and the peasant would fell and trim it.

The tree was installed in the dining room and decorated while I was in bed on Christmas Eve. Apart from baubles, the tree would be hung with real candles as we had no fairy lights nor electricity to run them. The base of the tree was covered with cotton wool for snow and a little doll's house, with windows and a candle inside, was placed at the base. On a bench outside the doll's house sat the old couple that live in a wood from Maeterlinck's play, The Blue Bird, a variation on Peter Pan. When we lived in Moscow, Mother once took me to a craft museum with a dazzling display of Christmas decorations for sale. I have never looked at Christmas decorations since without recalling that vision; those glinting, different coloured, glass balls.

Our presents were often notional since it was impossible to buy anything in the country of interest to children. We did however receive stockings with trifles in them and sometimes we were given tangerines but town guests brought more interesting gifts. From early morning, the dining room table was laid with decanters of vodka and whatever snacks were available. A procession of peasants came to congratulate us on the holiday. In addition to our usual peasant visitors, the chairman and secretary of the village committee invariably arrived. The chairman was a splendid looking, tall *mujik* with a well kept, long white beard. He spoke in measured, dignified tones and could have been easily taken for a somewhat pompous aristocrat. The secretary was much smaller, insignificant looking and, amusingly, totally illiterate. No women ever came. The peasants consumed vodka, not in small wine glasses but by the tumbler. Two tumblers was the usual ration and ours would not have been the first house they visited. But it had no visible effect on them; they might have been drinking water or milk.

*   *   *

Our manservant, Adam, was the local Don Juan. It was not unusual for my grandmother to say at breakfast, "Adam, a new child is born in the village, is it yours?"

"Not this time I assure you, Madam," Adam would answer.

Finally however, Adam decided to settle down and took as his bride the parlourmaid from the large house opposite ours, "Mamontov's dacha". When they married, she joined our staff and after that we had two maids.

I was best man and dressed for the occasion in my English suit. I set out with the bridegroom while someone else sat next to the driver holding high a sizable icon. A procession of the open carriages, used by the peasants to ferry summer visitors to their dachas, took us to the church. Since Adam was a Pole, he had no relations in Russia but the bride was blessed with at least fifty uncles, aunts and cousins who lived in neighbouring villages and all arrived for the wedding. I remember very little of the ceremony because I was mostly concerned about being too short to hold the crown over Adam's head. Fortunately in the event, someone saw my difficulty and held the crown for me.

A splendid lunch was provided for the peasants on the east terrace. My parents and other helpers served the long tables at which the servants were sitting with their guests. People raised their glasses and shouted, "*Gorka*," whereupon the bride and groom would have to kiss and thus it would go on. I sat next to a splendid *mujik* with a scarlet shirt and a long black beard. He asked me, "Do you drink?" and I said I did. So he provided me with a tumbler full of port. I had never drunk port before but liked the taste and I emptied the tumbler pretty smartly. Then I thought, "I'm getting a little sleepy, perhaps I'll go and rest," so I laid myself out and went to sleep. An hour later I woke up feeling perfectly fresh and went to watch them dancing to concertinas in the courtyard. To this day, I have not been to a more enjoyable wedding.

The next morning it was my duty as best man to wake the newly-weds by breaking something against the walls of their house. So I recruited the boy from next door and together we found a large number of flower-pots which we smashed noisily. The couple did not emerge however and there was a lot of mess to clear up.

I do not think we would have managed without Adam. For some reason he had been invalided out of the army but he never showed any sign of ill health. He came from a peasant family so he was able to do everything on the farming side. He was quite a handsome chap. Although he came from Poland, he was completely Russified and spoke with no accent. I used to visit him in his cottage in the yard and I think he was quite fond of me, as I was of him. Right to the end, until we left Russia when I was fourteen, Adam used to bath me. He would carry me to the bath, and put me in. Then he would soap and dry me and carry me back wrapped in a towel. I find this totally incredible now but then I do not think it ever occurred to me to bath myself.

The Shooting Party

My mother exerted a steadying influence, countering Father's enthusiasm with caution and more than once vetoed what she considered to be a dangerous or foolhardy plan. All projects concerning me required her stamp of approval and it was a red letter day when she consented to me accompanying Father on a shooting trip with his friends: Schmidt, the Commissar of Labour and Tomski, the Head of Trade Unions.

Although by this time Father had the use of more than one car, we travelled by train to Kashira, where we were met by Schmidt's Rolls Royce, a dark blue Silver Ghost with a long bonnet and open body. Cars were much more important in Russia after the Revolution than anyone would imagine nowadays. In England, after the last war, an old Rolls Royce was something of a status symbol but that was nothing in comparison to the attitude of the commissars. Only the best would do for them. Trotsky appropriated the Tsar's car, the French Delaune Belleville, recognisable by its circular radiator. Lenin had a Rolls Royce, now housed in the Lenin Museum. The other commissars competed for the best cars which they bought with foreign money. Tomski, for example, had a very smart, jet black, open car of the long forgotten American make, Pierce Arrow.

We travelled through fairly featureless countryside, mostly fields of rye, to an old estate which had been requisitioned and made into a state farm. It was still daylight when we arrived and the house, which must have been built in the nineteenth century or earlier, looked like something straight out of Chekhov. It was a two-storied wooden house, painted a faded grey, standing fairly high up above the river and surrounded by some woodland. The fields began nearly at the back door. Inside the house, there was almost no furniture and we spent most of our time, when indoors, in a very long room, which would be the ballroom in England and in Russia is called the *zala*. The only reminder of its former glory was a three-quarter size statue of a blackamoor. Part of the floor was covered in windfall apples. A rough table with some kitchen chairs completed the furnishings.

Schmidt's younger brother was the farm manager. He was quite good looking and lived in the house with his mother. He seemed to work reasonably hard and I do not think we saw him, even at meals. I remember him sitting on the front porch and dealing with a queue of labourers, handing out wages and instructions for the following day. I think that he was enthusiastic about his work, like many of the state farm managers, who believed that they were helping to build a new world based on new concepts and new relations. In this case, the farm was a requisitioned estate but later peasants' land was put into a collective state farm or *kolkhoz*. This enabled modern machinery to be used but turned the peasants into serfs, whereas previously they had been independent farmers. The *kolkhoz* workers were tied to the land. They could not leave their farms because their passports would not allow them to do so. Before the communist regime, a peasant could leave his village and work in town if he wanted to. As in the village of Listviani, the land was shared by the peasants in a collective or *mir* which was administered by the elders. This situation continued for some time after the Revolution, before state collectivization took hold. The state farms were based on an entirely artificial system, as were the state enterprises. Had things been properly costed, it would have been clear that they sold their produce at a considerable loss. But when a state farm made a loss, it still continued to function as though nothing had happened.

Schmidt's mother was a neat little woman, born in Russia of German or Volga German parents. The Volga Germans had been imported by Catherine the Great to colonise the wide open spaces of White Russia and to set an example to the Russians of how to be tidy, farm well and stay sober. True to his heritage, Schmidt never showed the slightest sign of inebriation. He was a reserved character, modest, well-mannered and dignified. Like my papa he was always carefully dressed and we all respected him. He came from a poor family (I remember something being said about his mother having worked as a cook) and, despite his natural self-restraint, he openly enjoyed the perks of his position. Schmidt and his wife used to stay with us in the country and on one occasion Father, Schmidt and I were walking somewhere near to our dacha when we met the local *militsinier*. I had never seen the policeman before but Father knew him and introduced him to Schmidt, without telling him that Schmidt was the Commissar of Labour. Schmidt said, "Well do you take bribes?"

"Are you joking?" the *militsinier* replied, "Of course I take bribes. How can I live without them?" This amused the Commissar considerably.

Schmidt was executed by Stalin. By that time we were living in England and it was reported in the London papers. But originally he had been in Stalin's inner circle and when it looked as though there might be a communist revolution in Germany, he was sent to assist the revolutionaries, presumably travelling with false papers. My papa, of course, made no attempt to be a comrade and never hid his views. He felt very firmly that the communist ideas were nonsense and would not work. But Schmidt was not aggressively enthusiastic and their friendship was not affected. On this trip, I do not remember any political discussion taking place at all.

Mealtimes were enjoyable although the food, prepared by Schmidt's mother, was modest and in no way memorable. Tomski was a middle-aged man whose face clearly bore the consequence of too much drink. As the

Russians say, he was 'no fool with the bottle' and he consumed endless glasses of vodka both at lunch and dinner. He was easy-going, likable and pleasant to everyone. He enjoyed telling us jokes and was unperturbed by the fact that even I, at the age of twelve, had heard the majority of his repertoire before. In addition to Schmidt and Tomski, the party included Schmidt's brother-in-law, a distant relative of my mother's. He was a boy of seventeen or eighteen with heavy Jewish features and very dark hair. He was supposed to be helping with the harvest on the state farm but was clearly out of his element and was much teased by the peasants, particularly the young women. The drivers also used to eat with us although they were not allowed any vodka. This practice of having the drivers at the table was common amongst communist ministers. It was not our custom, although nowadays when I go to Russia, I invite my driver to eat with me when dining out in Moscow.

In the mornings, I went out with the transport, which was horse-drawn, to load hay. I am afraid I was not of much assistance since the bales were very heavy but the farm girls who were very high spirited and in some cases quite pretty, made quite a fuss of me. They did not overstrain themselves and joked constantly. On the way back, the men let me drive, or rather sit on the horse when the hay was being taken to the store house. One poor girl was constantly teased and called "the Armenian's wife". The meaning of this became clearer when Schmidt took Father and me to visit a neighbouring state farm managed by a young Armenian. I think Schmidt wanted to show off the speed of the horse for we travelled in an open carriage instead of the Rolls Royce. Father and I sat in the carriage while Schmidt sat in the coachman's seat and drove. The horse was highly bred and I was thrilled to be sitting behind such a fine animal. The Armenian lived in an English-style brick house surrounded by endless fields of rye. When we arrived, he produced tea and vodka and sat down with a balalaika to give us a recital of well known Russian folk songs.

The shooting itself proved to be a complete fiasco and very nearly finished badly for me. I was used as a beater to rouse the partridge in the fields. This involved striking at the undergrowth with a long stick and I set about my task with vigour. In fact, there turned out to be no partridge at all but Tomski, who was very short-sighted, saw some movement and discharged both barrels in my direction. Fortunately he was also short-sighted enough to miss. Afterwards, he insisted that we must bag some game and quite matter-of-factly shot a number of sparrows that were on the ground. We ate them for dinner that evening and they tasted quite delicious.

Schmidt offered to drive Father and me back to Moscow in his Rolls Royce and unwisely we accepted. We set off early in the evening but the quality of the Soviet inner tubes was appalling and every few miles we had a burst tyre. At first the inner tubes were replaced but when all the spares had been used, the punctures had to be patched. We did not reach Moscow until the early hours of the morning by which time it was obviously too late for us to continue our journey to Mamontovka. So Schmidt invited us to stay at his quarters in the Kremlin.

In those days, the Kremlin was closed to the public and heavily guarded. Having passed several sentry posts, we arrived at some fairly steep steps leading up to one of the entrances. I was carrying a melon which had been given to me as a present and I was nearly at the top of the steps when it slipped out of my hands and rolled towards a group of sentries standing below. Of course in the dark, it looked like a bomb and caused considerable excitement. As soon as we arrived, Schmidt was told that he and Tomski were expected by Stalin for dinner. It was two o'clock in the morning. Stalin, of course, functioned largely at night.

Moscow School

In the autumn of 1922, my parents decided that I had outgrown the village school mistress' range of subjects and that I should go to school in Moscow. They chose the Ninth People's School, which before the Revolution had been a private school called the Gymnasia Flerova, and Mother took me to Moscow for the entrance examination. I had not been to Moscow for several years but very little seemed to have changed. When we arrived at the Northern station there was the usual wild crowd of *izvorshchiks* getting hold of us and pulling. After a bit of a scene we agreed a price and got a cab. Another *izvorshchik* shouted after us, "Don't go with him. His horse has tuberculosis. You'll never get there."

The school was housed in quite a smart building and although it had been purpose built, it looked more like a very large house than an educational establishment. The site must have been too small to build the great hall on the ground floor so it was on the top floor instead. It was quite ornate and could have been mistaken for a ballroom in a private house, except for the small stage on which they used to put a platform for meetings.

All the candidates were accompanied by th r mothers and a slight row developed between the porter and a very heav built woman who had used the men's lavatory. The porter, who remained from the old times, maintained that ladies should know which door to use. Mother found herself sitting next to a Polish Jewish woman from Warsaw whose surname was Unshlicht and who turned out to be the wife of the second-in-command of the *Cheka* (later called the KGB). Her son was a good-looking, well-bred boy and as we say in Russian, clearly not the descendant of any peasant. At that point, he was not fully aware of his father's importance and was quite pleasant. The examination itself was fairly summary. We were tested on Russian writing and reading and had to do some basic arithmetic on the blackboard. I made a mistake in one of the calculations but was helped to correct it and I was told that I had passed.

We returned to the dacha in the early evening and a discussion began about where I would stay in Moscow since, despite having a free pass on the railway, it was thought impractical for me to commute from Mamontovka every day. The choice fell on Milia, the youngest and probably the nicest of all Mother's half sisters. Like most of Grandfather's first brood, Milia was fair, almost a Scandinavian blonde, as was her daughter Genia. Her husband, Mikhail Kovarski, was in the paper business and they lived in the same block that my mother had lived in as a child, although they had a totally different standard of living. Their flat was very modest and for that reason had not been requisitioned, but they had been made to give up their spare room to a young couple. This couple also shared the kitchen with them, or more accurately with their old nanny who both cooked and slept in the kitchen. There was not, therefore, a separate room for me, nor for that matter a bed. They put several chairs together in the living room, threw a mattress over them and that was where I slept. During the night, the chairs would shift and every so often I would find myself on the floor.

I did not stay very long with Aunt Milia and went instead to live with Father's second cousin Nadia who was very beautiful and quite young. She was newly married to a somewhat doubtful character who had trained as an opera singer but had become a nepman with a brass plate on the door giving his profession as a broker. He later introduced some private capital into Standard Trust, the conglomerate that my father headed. Staying with Nadia was not ideal. The flat was quite large and newly decorated but I still did not have a room of my own and slept on a divan in the sitting room. There were also too many guests and the atmosphere was somewhat volatile. One evening the man in charge of the block of flats arrived with a female student intending to requisition the maid's room for the young woman to live in. A row developed between the manager and Nadia's brother-in-law who was visiting. The manager took offence at something the brother-in-law said and fetched a policeman who came in a Balaclava helmet, covered in snow, to hear the insult repeated. However the brother-in-law refused to oblige and when asked where he lived, replied, "In Moscow," and then disappeared. Another time, Nadia's husband was arrested and Nadia phoned my father who arrived in the evening. Unfortunately Father was suffering from an infected abscess in his mouth and had a high temperature. I managed to develop bronchitis at the same time. So Nadia gave up her bed and the two of us were laid out on the two beds in the bedroom. After a day or two, however Father, went out and managed to get Nadia's husband released.

This incident convinced Father that I had to have a flat of my own. There was a dreadful shortage of accommodation in Moscow and Father had people rushing around looking out for possibilities. One suggestion was a town house occupied by nine girls of ill repute. Father thought that he could succeed in having them turned out but failed. Then he decided to build, which was a possibility because Standard Trust had a building concern among its companies. He began to design a house, to be built of wood and which in its preliminary sketches looked narrow and tall like an English house in Knightsbridge. However, even with Father's drive and connections, getting a site in central Moscow proved too difficult.

Eventually, through a partner of Nadia's husband called Asarch, a flat was found for me in a small, very attractive, early nineteenth century house. It was situated next to the Pushkin Museum, originally called the Museum of

Alexander III and faced the cathedral, which is now being rebuilt after Stalin demolished it in the '30s. By Soviet standards, the flat was magnificent. There was a very long and pretty sitting room leading to a balcony bedroom for me, a bedroom for the parents when they were there, a maid's room, a kitchen and a bathroom. The bathroom however had to be shared with Asarch's sister who lived with a female friend in a large single room. Tante Sophie's furniture was taken out of store and installed at the flat. It was all antique and included a complete William and Mary dining room with twelve chairs and two side boards, some Louis XV pieces with marquetry and some Chippendale. In 1981, I visited the Museum of the Donskoi Monastery with my wife and younger daughter. Almost the first exhibit I saw was one of my chairs labelled, "English work".

Thus, at the age of thirteen, I was installed in the centre of town with a retainer to cook and look after me. My parents spent some time in the flat and I went back to the country for weekends but I was alone for a good deal of the time. However, I did not feel a stranger or in any way abandoned or lonely. I liked the city. The Russian male, when he had had enough to drink, would open his window and, sitting with his legs dangling outside the building, would play the concertina and sing for his own enjoyment. Moscow had not changed very much. Some of the streets had been renamed which caused a great deal of confusion and some people refused to use the new names. The police had revolvers but they were not particularly aggressive. Everyone carried passports but most people would have carried them before the Revolution. I went back to school during NEP so there was no greater shortage of food in the shops than now. The school itself was relatively well equipped, well maintained and warm. The difficult years came later.

The school was in the middle of town and the playground was so small that, at break times, we had to be let out class by class. The school itself was run in two shifts, due to lack of space and I belonged to the senior shift which arrived at two o'clock. Before school, I was tutored by one of the masters called Nikolai Nikolaievich. He came every morning and then had lunch with me. I think he became quite fond of me and I have an affectionate letter that he wrote to me when I was in England in which he complained that I was beginning to make mistakes when writing in Russian. His wife was an actress at the Arts Theatre so before the Revolution she must have earned substantially more than him. He cared about my doing well without pushing me hard. I was probably the only boy in the school who had a private tutor but my papa did not like to take chances. I had to get on and fortunately I did reasonably well.

After I had been at the school for six months, the Dalton System was introduced. This allowed pupils to work at their own pace and was very successful. The school was divided into subject rooms known as laboratories.

So there was a laboratory of Russian, of History, of Mathematics and so on, except for languages which were taught in the ordinary way. We were each given a record card with all our subjects printed on it and the teachers set us work for a month, during which time we had to read certain books or in the case of Mathematics, solve certain problems. Our first Mathematics assignment under the Dalton System was to discover all the trigonometric relations for ourselves by drawing triangles, measuring them and finding out what we could about sine, cosine and so on. Of course it would have taken far too long to make all these calculations and the project had to be dropped. But the new system soon settled down and ideas about how much work we could get through in a month became more realistic. At the end of each month, or earlier if you felt ready, you took examinations. If you passed, the master would sign your record card and you could then go on to the next stage. You could make an appointment with a master to be examined at any time and if you worked, it was possible to get well ahead. There were other advantages to the new system as far as the pupils were concerned. If we sat and talked to our friends in the laboratory, it was assumed that we were exchanging important information; we were not even expected to look as though we were working. The system was not, however, infallible and one boy in my class made great progress on the Dalton system by forging signatures.

To begin with, I used to take a cab to school. I had tried travelling by tram once or twice but was discouraged. They were so full that you had to fight to get on and there was a high risk of catching something from people breathing straight at you. Besides, my papa did not like the idea of his son using public transport. Later the conglomerate's cars took me to school and fetched me and, in the winter, the conglomerate provided a sleigh with a rather splendid black horse. The conglomerate's garage had many cars, none of which worked particularly well. They had all been assembled from parts of different makes. Thus the radiator said Talbot and the hub caps said Renault. There were quite a few open cars but the cars that used to take me to school were closed cars with partitions. One driver was a Cossack with huge arm muscles. There was one particular car, an enormously long, open, pale blue limousine made in a factory called Russian Baltic which required all his strength to turn the wheel. There were always two drivers because the cars used to break down fairly frequently. You could not leave a car in Moscow even for a moment without it being stripped, so one of the drivers would wait with the car while the other telephoned for help. When this happened, I would not wait for the car to be repaired but used to take a horse cab home. That was quite an amusing exercise. I would look for the most presentable horses and then having chosen a cab on this basis, gave the address. The *izvorshchik* then named a sum. Before the stabilization of the currency, he would ask for at least a million. You paid no attention to this and walked on. The cab driver would follow, asking whether you realised how much a sack of oats cost, how many children he had and so forth. Still you paid no attention. After a while he would say, "All right, half a million"

"Four hundred thousand"

"Get in."

Business was always conducted in this manner. There was no foreign currency in Russia after the Revolution so inflation could not be described in terms of so many roubles to the dollar but nevertheless it could be calculated from price increases. In May 1922, railway fares were one million times what they had been in 1917. They doubled in June and again in the Autumn. Inflation ended in 1923 with the issue of a new currency called *chervonetz*. This followed the gold standard and proved to be more or less stable. While Father was in England in '23, Mother and I went to have a photograph taken of us to send to him. A senior official from the Ministry of Finance happened to be at the studio at the same time. The photographer asked him, "Well, is this new currency going to keep its value?" The official replied, "With my signature on it, of course it will."

When the conglomerate's car did not arrive to take me to school, I would telephone the Transport Manager and ask, "Where is my car?" After listening to excuses about the difficulties of getting tyres and so on, I would take a horse cab or sleigh, bargaining with the driver as usual. The *izvorshchiks* were quite amusing. They used to ask, "What are you studying?" "Do you know where one's soul is?" I am afraid I was not much help in this direction.

My piano teacher used to come to teach me at my flat but I soon went on strike because I had enough to do without his lessons. He had thick grey hair and always wore the same unfashionable corduroy suit. He was an accomplished musician and, before the Revolution, used to give small recitals in the houses of wealthy patrons but he completely failed to handle me properly and I thought he was a great bore. There was no radio, so after school, I had my dinner and either did my homework or read. I do not remember ever issuing out on my own. On one occasion, there was a film show at school. I chose the second showing which was supposed to start at eight or nine o'clock but the first showing had finished late because the film kept on breaking. My cook-general came to fetch me and, by the time we left to look for a horse cab and sleigh, it was half past one in the morning. To my amazement, a cab was available and off we went. Being driven, wrapped in furs, by a fast horse in a sleigh through snow in Moscow was an immensely satisfying sensation.

I travelled on the train by myself quite a bit because I used to return to Mamontovka every weekend. On the trains, there was a continual procession of *bisprisorne*, neglected children who slept on the streets and in the back of vans. They normally came singly and would look around to determine what kind of public it was. If it did not appear excessively communist, they would sing and I think people normally gave them something. Generally they had their own song;

"Here I am abandoned, an orphan, with no one to look after me,
And I will die before long and there will be no one to pray at my grave,
Only the nightingale will sing occasionally on the nearest tree."

I remember one boy accompanying himself on a concertina. Occasionally they would do an anti-regime thing;-

"Before I was a thief who picked people's pockets
But now I have become a Commissar."

I was once returning to the country when I noticed a man dressed in denim, which was only worn by workmen in those days. The ticket collector came round, looked at his ticket and said, "It's no good.".

"Why is it no good?" asked the workman.

"The train does not stop at this station."

"Oh."

"Well, you will have to pay the fare to the next station."

The workman said, "I'm sorry. I haven't got any money" and a discussion took place between the ticket collector and his colleague. Suddenly the workman stood up, shook off the collector, pulled the communication cord and jumped into a field of rye while the train was still moving. The ticket collector took out his revolver and attempted unsuccessfully to shoot the workman down. It is incredible that shooting could start over something as trifling as the fare between two stations but I was there and it happened.

Father used to enjoy recounting the schoolboy pranks of his friends but the atmosphere was very different when I went to school. It was not the time for practical jokes. Yet the political atmosphere in the school was far from orthodox and some traditions still persisted from pre-Revolutionary times when the school had been private. About half the staff, including Nikolai Nikolaievich, were openly anti-Bolshevik and still wore tailcoats, wing-collars, starched shirts and black tie; the other half were dressed *à la* Stalin. The pupils on the Communist Committee of the school once disgraced themselves by getting drunk in the small ballroom. The walls were splashed with vodka and there was broken glass everywhere. Needless to say, they lost their position on the committee and were expelled.

Automatic obedience to Communist organisations had not yet reached our school. One day we were called to a meeting with several pupils on the platform including Unshlicht, the son of the second in command of Cheka. A man stood up and proposed a list of pupils to be elected to the school committee. An uproar broke out and people shouted, "Get down. No one has elected you. Who the hell are you? We don't want you." But that was the last demonstration of independence for a long time. A few years later and the protesters would have disappeared.

We saw very little of the headmaster and, on occasions when speeches had to be made, one of the other masters did the usual panegyric. This master could have passed quite easily for a painter. He had a small very tidy beard and wore neither a tailcoat nor the communist jacket known as a French but a normal suit jacket with trousers that did not match. He had a rather plump secretary who, according to some of the boys, was considerably more than a secretary to him. But apart from seeing this elegant figure in the corridors and sitting on the platform on occasions such as Lenin's death, he made no impact on me whatever.

My Russian master was quite elderly and his garb was neither Communist nor old guard. I think he was the only one on the premises to wear an ordinary suit. He used to sit in the laboratory and was available to answer questions. However he spent most of his time examining people, so one could work nearby and overhear what he asked. Once I overheard him examining another boy on Turgenev's 'Fathers and Sons'. One of the questions he asked was, "By what street did Bazarov leave Moscow?" I listened to the answer and when he examined me, of course I replied immediately and he complimented me on how thoroughly I had read the book.

Our form mistress was the only Jewish member of staff. She dressed neatly, perhaps a little severely and we called her by her name and patronymic, Iliena Mikhailovna. She was not very effective. The French mistress had a weird appearance like a joke elderly governess. Being very plump, she did not appear to have legs and she had a funny face. She was never addressed by her name and patronymic but invariably known as Mademoiselle. The Biology mistress was fairly ample, had pleasant face and wore her hair in a bun. She taught a combination of Biology, Zoology and Botany in a very well equipped laboratory with an aquarium, plants and the like. Her lessons were quite interesting and inspired me to pick up a small snake that I saw on the pavement on my way to school. I did not know anything about snakes but I was wearing gloves and it did not seem to be too worried or to try to get away from me. It had dark spots and may have been a small adder and I brought it to the Biology mistress, instead of chocolates.

But the person who had most influence on me was the Maths and Physics master. He was dark-haired, fairly tall and wore a communist jacket. He was hardly ever sarcastic but very sure of himself and very good with us. I was not yet in the habit of standing up whenever a master approached me so the first time he went round the form and looked at my work, he gently levered me up by the elbow. Of course, I went on doing this in England and, on my first day at University College School, I jumped up the moment a master appeared, only to find that everyone else had remained seated. The Maths and Physics master made his subject interesting and we participated in his endeavours. For the school Physics exhibition I made a chemical rectifier with some cooking implement made of clay or porcelain, a solution and two plates. I also made a rudimentary arc light, which I could run off the rectifier, from carbons pulled out of large old fashioned batteries. It gave off a brilliant light and proved to be my friends' favourite entertainment in my flat. Father was abroad most of the time I spent in my flat, and we exchanged letters. In one of them, I described the chemical rectifier and arc lamp. Father replied that he had shown my design to a very senior man at Marconi and that they had jointly approved it.

The school was co-educational but, without any ruling from the authorities, the girls sat on one side of the classroom and the boys on the other. There was a quite pretty, somewhat plump Jewish girl with whom I thought I was in love but I never tried to make her acquaintance. The Revolution mixed us up socially to a far greater extent than any comprehensive school. My three best friends were the sons respectively of a percussionist at the Bolshoi Theatre, a tram conductor and a garage mechanic. I was privileged above and beyond all the other pupils at the school with the exception of Unshlicht who lived in the Kremlin. Needless to say, with my father's lack of a sense of proportion, I was over-endowed with pocket money. I did not have to pay for anything, except the occasional fare for a horse cab when the car failed to turn up, and my prosperity was soon discovered by the pupils who used to ask me to lend them money now and again. Mostly, I got it back but then one of the girls caught onto the idea and that time I do not think I was repaid. One boy decided that we had to go and buy Finnish knives, the sort used to kill people or animals. I did not really see the need for such a weapon but I did buy one, although I do not remember what happened to it.

I had no real grasp of social differences and I did not understand that when the tram conductor's son and the garage mechanic's son visited me in my flat next to the Pushkin Museum, they would be totally overcome and deprived of the power of speech. There I was in a three bedroom flat, with antique furniture, in one of the best parts of Moscow, being served by a maid while they lived in a single room, with their parents, siblings and probably a grandparent. I do not think that they could believe their eyes. But I had no idea of the disparity until I called on my best friend who had a Ukrainian name and whose father was the percussion player in the Bolshoi orchestra. One might have thought that it would be a reasonably well paid job but the family lived in a single room. My friend was an only child so there were three beds, one of which was not made. That really quite shook me. My friend came to visit me in the country. He was academically quite capable. But after a little while, the people with educated parents mixed more with each other than with the others. One of my friends, called Weinberg, was of Swedish origin and his sister was blonde. They lived in a flat opposite the school in the centre of Moscow and they were clearly "former people." I think they may have had a dacha somewhere near ours and I saw quite a lot of him. We went to an exhibition at which Father's conglomerate had a pavilion. The manager of the pavilion did not know me at all but when I gave my name they made an enormous fuss of us and I remember walking round this exhibition with my friend and his sister in long pigtails. Their father had previously been a banker and during NEP started up some kind of a bank near to where they lived. The bank kept a horse and carriage to take the father to work since it is a Russian tradition, to this day, that people of sufficient seniority do not use public transport.

For a long time we were given no political instruction whatsoever. But a government inspection made the headmaster decide that something had to be done to make us aware of the changed times, and there was an attempt to involve us with the city of Moscow by making us write reports on municipal services. We were allowed to choose which service to write about and naturally I chose telephones since telephony had been my papa's occupation. Unfortunately, however, telephones were considered to come under the topic of electricity which someone else had chosen and I was left, quite literally, with the drains. I could not get any help from my father on drains so I went to the city library, took out a couple of pamphlets and discovered how many hundred miles of lead pipes, clay pipes and wooden pipes there were in Moscow and wrote that up. At the beginning of my lecture I said, "My subject may appear to you very undistinguished but I ask you, what can you do without drains?" That went down well and then I recited the mileage of the different pipes. We were also taken to the Historical Museum which is just off Red Square and we had to carry out traffic surveys, noting how many cars, horse drawn carriages and so forth passed this way and that. It never occurred to me that I should assimilate the Communist background and there was no pressure on me to do so. I do not remember ever trying to pass myself off as a comrade.

At the end of my first year at school, I caught pneumonia. I was too ill even to leave the school and the German mistress called Lydia Germanovna gave up her small room and her bed and there I stayed for a month. Dr Shapiro called regularly; to begin with twice a day and later daily. There were no antibiotics in those days and they used mustard plasters and bound my chest. It was not a pleasant experience. I remember having acute headaches and lying in bed feeling ill and dull. Lydia Germanovna practically nursed me. She was not particularly young but very pleasant looking, with blonde hair and blue eyes, and always very neatly dressed. Her room was in a small pavilion in the courtyard of the school. This pavilion was also occupied by the senior master and by the widow and daughter of the proprietor of the original Gymnasia Flerova. The senior master was of German origin but was called Sakharov. I suppose his name had originally been Zucher, meaning sugar, or Zucherman and he russified it during the First World War when German names became unfashionable. Lydia Germanovna's room was approached through a common room on the first floor of the building where they all had meals and it overlooked the courtyard so, when I was slightly better, I could watch the pupils being let out to play.

The end of a Russian winter is very dramatic. The snow begins to melt, water pours all over the place and little green shoots start popping out. There is an incredible feeling of spring and it is curious but, when I was ill in this house overlooking the playground, I sensed it spontaneously without going out. As a result of my illness, I missed the end of year examinations which I would have passed with no difficulty had I been at school. Father went to see the headmaster, told him that he would consider it totally unacceptable for me to stay down a year and asked for two masters to be sent to the country to examine me. The headmaster agreed that this was an entirely practicable suggestion but asked Father whether he was aware of the school's pressing need to be painted inside and out. If Father's conglomerate would see to this matter, the two masters would be sent to examine me. Father agreed. The school was duly repainted and two masters arrived at the dacha, one of whom was the Mathematics and Physics master. I passed the examination very easily and they were each given an elaborate foreign pen-knife with everything on it, including an instrument to disgorge hooks from fish.

When I was twelve or thirteen, Father and I went to a Jewish tailor to be measured for new fur coats. We went down into the basement where the tailor and his wife lived and worked. I had never before come across a provincial Jewish craftsman and he seemed quite alien to me, no different from a gypsy. The basement opened onto a courtyard and, no sooner had we arrived, than some boys came up to the lower windows and started yelling at the tailor and his wife, "Damned Yids." This quite upset them and they shouted to the boys to go away. My papa ignored it completely. He felt that the insult did not apply to him one little bit and he did not mention it to me afterwards because he fully expected people who spoke Yiddish, or very heavily accented Russian, to be considered "damned Yids".

I think it was in the summer of '22 that I was taken to have my adenoids removed. As far as I remember, I did not have to wait but went immediately into a largish room where there were already about five other boys and two bearded men, who appeared to be directing the proceedings. They turned out to be a professor of medicine and his assistant, whose function was to hold us on his knees while the operation took place. I was the first and the professor peered inside my mouth and said, "Let's see, let's see." Then he painted the area to be attacked with what was perhaps a local anaesthetic, pushed with a steel instrument and a bit of meat fell onto my tongue. He did the other side in the same way and then, as if he were saying "Next for shaving", the professor called for the next boy. I sat down to watch the other chaps being operated on. When the next boy had been done, he was put on a chair and immediately fell down in a faint. This did not seem to cause any surprise. At some point, I asked how soon I would be able to play tennis and received the answer, "Well, you won't feel like it for a few days but when you feel like it, why shouldn't you play?" Then I was handed over to my father who, quite atypically, had accompanied me. We drove in an open car to the station, took the train back to Mamontovka and then walked the short distance to the dacha. I was not put to bed but reclined on the sofa in the study, feeling worse and worse as time passed.

Aunt Sonia and Uncle Vitia

Mother's elder sister Sonia, or Tante Sophie as she was known to me, had a very warm personality. She was much more outgoing than my mother and more demonstrative but lacked her self-control. She was quite spoilt, demanding and somewhat lacking in tact compared with my mama, but it was difficult not to be fond of her.

In spite of my father's warnings, Sonia married his cousin Vitia Poliakoff. Vitia was extremely good-looking, a great dandy and a tremendous snob. Sonia told me that he was madly jealous and capable of making dreadful scenes. Once, when they were at the Bolshoi Theatre, he accused her of staring at a man in a box a considerable distance from theirs. Sonia meanwhile had no idea which box or which man Vitia was talking about.

Vitia qualified as an engineer at a university in St Petersburg but was hopelessly misguided in what he wanted to achieve in life. He was forever expecting to become a millionaire and was always engaged in deals which never really succeeded. He had the mind of the businessmen who sat about in cafés in Odessa and sold carloads of goods to each other. There is a joke that a man comes into the café and they ask him, "How are you?" He says, "I've got diabetes." This news is passed on, he's got lots of diabetes, next he's got a carload of diabetes and they start selling each other carloads of diabetes.

I do not remember seeing Aunt Sonia and Uncle Vitia together very much, although Vitia used to visit us quite often because he relied on my grandfather to finance his various operations. Looking through a drawer a long time after the Revolution, I discovered a large number of bills of exchange that he had made out to Grandfather but which clearly he had never paid. One day, Uncle Vitia came to my grandfather and said, "There's a block of flats for sale at a very good price. Why don't you buy it?" Grandfather asked the price and then, without seeing the property, agreed to pay ten percent less. But the block of flats was old and a child standing at one of the windows fell out, together with the window frame. Fortunately she landed on a pair of cart-horses delivering beer and there was no injury although the horses must have got quite a fright. The police came to see Grandfather who was the landlord and told him that it was disgraceful that he should own a block of flats that fell to bits. So Grandfather told Vitia to sell the flats which he managed to do for twenty thousand roubles more than they had paid for it. Vitia came back and said, "Well, you haven't done anything, have you? So I'll keep the twenty thousand."

Uncle Vitia had an old university friend called Burde. After we arrived in England, Burde appeared, in a light blue Rolls Royce, accompanied by a Russian woman secretary. He had become an arms salesman for Vickers and successor to Sir Basil Zaharov who had been infamous for his bribing methods. Wanting to secure an arms contract in Russia, Zaharov called at the house of the General who was in charge of awarding the contract. As he expected, the General was not at home and Zaharov was received by the General's wife. After some polite conversation he suddenly looked up at a very ordinary, even miserable chandelier and said, "What a wonderful specimen, the rarest chandelier I have ever seen. I collect them, Madame. Could your manservant perhaps bring a pair of steps to allow me to examine it more closely?" After climbing up and pretending to give the chandelier a thorough inspection, he came down the steps and said, "A marvellous piece of luck, Madame. This is just what is missing from my collection. Would you be kind enough to ask His Excellency, the General, whether he would accept 100,000 roubles for this unique piece of art?" The General accepted and Zaharov got the contract, and it soon became clear from Burde's chatter that he too thought that bribery was the only way to do business.

Leaving Russia

On 21st January 1924, the traffic in Moscow went on all night. My mother was staying with me at my flat opposite the Pushkin Museum and, in the morning, we learnt that Lenin was dead. At school, a meeting was called in the great hall; most of the masters were there and we heard several, long speeches. The next thing I remember is coming home for the holidays. Father had been abroad for a month or more on a mission to the West finishing in London. We went to the station, with Schmidt and someone from the conglomerate, to meet him. Father was wearing a pair of highly polished brown shoes, such as we had not seen for some time.

In London, Father had resumed his friendship with Godfrey Isaacs, the Managing Director of Marconi, and introduced him to the Russian Ambassador, Rakovski. When Father returned to Russia he realised that he stood a very good chance of being shot, because the atmosphere had changed abruptly after Lenin's death. I had not noticed the change because there were no visible signs. But returning to the conglomerate, Father could feel the spreading fear. He sent a telegram to Godfrey Isaacs with the message in English, "Must leave here at once" and the same day, Isaacs went to see the Russian Ambassador. He asked for my father to be sent urgently to London to discuss building Marconi Radio Stations in Russia because he was the only man who understood local conditions. The Ambassador then sent a telegram to the Commissar of Labour who wrote on it, "I do not object" and thus my Father obtained his exit visa. Since Marconi clearly did not need me, aged thirteen, to help them with the design of radio stations, I was taken to a hospital and, in return for a bottle of French brandy, received a certificate stating that I would not survive another Russian winter. This was supported by the fact that I had suffered quite severe pneumonia the year before, the effects of which still showed.

My father and I left Russia in June 1924. He was leaving forever and I would only return forty-two years later. Mother, Adam and our driver and his wife came to see us off. Mother was unable to leave Russia because her father was seriously ill, but in any case it would have been hard to obtain an exit visa for her at this stage because Father was ostensibly going to England on a short term contract. By the time she came to England, Father was employed as Deputy Director of the Technical Department of the Russian Trade Delegation and was therefore allowed to bring his wife to England because he was likely to be based there for some years.

The clocks of the Northern Station and the station opposite it differed by exactly two minutes. In Shakespeare's words, the time was out of joint. But nobody wondered at this circumstance, for it had always been so and the discrepancy was attributed to a quarrel between the two station masters. Indeed everything, on this extraordinary day, was just as usual. The square outside the Moscow Terminus of the Northern Railway was full of horse cabs and we waited calmly for cabs to be hired to transfer us and our luggage to Riga Station. I do not think we were saying very much. Father's driver bargained with three cab drivers in their long blue coats and red sashes. As always, the drivers pointed out the rising costs of oats, the fact that they had a family to feed and then asked two or three times as much as the price for which they would finally settle. This was a well established ritual. Eventually, three cabs drew up to where we were standing and the drivers immediately defaulted on their agreement. More bargaining took place and we got into the cabs. The driver said plaintively to Father, "The moment they saw you, they asked for more." At Riga station, Father and I were put with all our luggage into what, before the Revolution, would have been a first class sleeper for two. Mother displayed tremendous self control and I do not remember any scenes. Kisses were exchanged and then we were off.

The train was slow and the journey to the border took several days. We passed through unfamiliar suburbs of Moscow, then monotonous landscape, broken only by the occasional miserable looking village. At these stops, the names of which I had never encountered before and do not now remember, peasant women, wrapped in shawls, rushed to the windows selling things to eat: curd cheese, buns and bits of cooked chicken. As we got nearer to the border, we saw male peasants, large men with long beards, standing about on the platforms. To my eye, they were doing nothing but Father told me that most of them were engaged in smuggling foreign goods and drink across the border.

Finally we arrived at the frontier station with Lithuania. Father strode onto the platform and demanded to see the head of the frontier police. A man in military uniform appeared and immediately took Father to be English which was not surprising since we were both clad from head to foot in clothes that Father had bought in Harrods the previous year. After disabusing the officer about our nationality, Father handed him a letter from the Commissar of Labour. It said that Father was on an important mission to London and asked them not to delay us at luggage inspection longer than was strictly necessary. The officer told us that they were not quite ready to start the luggage inspection and suggested that we adjourn to the restaurant and have some tea. Meanwhile all the luggage was taken off the train which was thoroughly searched because it was continuing across the Lithuanian border. In the restaurant I noticed a middle-aged Jewish couple. The man was well dressed, although his hair was quite long; the woman was plump and rather untidy with the Bohemian appearance of an unsuccessful painter. She had just been searched and was telling her husband that "all was well." I assumed from this that she had successfully concealed something from the customs officials.

Before long, we were called to the platform where all the luggage was lying together. Our cases were initialled and came from Aspreys in London. The dressing-case was made of crocodile leather and contained silver mounted jars, brushes and combs. In addition to the cases, there were Father's golf clubs and fishing rods but his shotguns had been left behind. All in all, our luggage stood out from other people's which consisted mostly of baskets, bundles and similar makeshift containers. Father's confident air must have concealed some anxiety for, like most people crossing the border, I knew we were smuggling a fairly large diamond, hidden in the lining of a little stud box in Father's dressing case. Our trunks, crammed with linen table cloths, antique Russian porcelain and silver seemed to be of no interest to the customs officials but the golf clubs puzzled them. Father tried to explain what they were but still they did not understand so he produced a ball and demonstrated on the platform. The customs men seemed disappointed and expressed disbelief that grown men should amuse themselves by knocking little balls about with sticks. "You can never tell what the English get up to!" they said. Owing to the letter, our luggage was not inspected thoroughly and, unlike a number of our fellow passengers, we were not taken to be searched. We returned to our carriage and the train crossed the border. I felt relieved and for the moment unworried about the future. Yet we were going to England with nothing arranged, no job and only one diamond.

As we left Russia travelling first into Lithuania, then into Latvia, the scenery changed remarkably. The village huts became houses, far superior to the wretched peasant dwellings in Russia and everything appeared altogether neater and cleaner. Inside the train, the atmosphere became very relaxed but conversation did not really start until we were in Germany when many people began exchanging their life stories.

The Russian railway track was built wider than the European standard gauge in order to slow down invading armies. But we did not have to change trains because the countries we went through had been part of the original Russian Empire. Eventually we arrived in Berlin where we were met by Aunt Sonia and Mouma and were taken to a substantial boarding house by taxi. The taxis at that time had curious torpedo shaped bodies and displayed a broken yellow stripe to distinguish them from other vehicles. Years later when visiting Berlin for a Trade Association meeting, I found the boarding house on Kurfürstendamm still standing when practically everything else around had been demolished and rebuilt.

Mouma had become a precocious teenager. She was smartly dressed, wearing the then fashionable chamber-pot hat which almost covered her eyes. She seemed plumper than before. She told me later that she was often approached by men which she found rather amusing. Her father turned up presently, his usual immaculate self in a grey Homburg hat, cane and spats, looking very prosperous although he was not. He was at the time living with his girlfriend but we were not to know this until later. A bank in Berlin held the bulk of the family jewels. I still do not know when or how they got there. I assumed that we would be given a share of the jewels to assist us in London but when I suggested this to Mouma she was horrified, saying that without the jewels they had nothing to live on.

We left Berlin after a few days, taking a train to the Hook of Holland. We shared a compartment with an elderly lady and her two daughters who were in their late twenties and very presentable. They were Russian Jews on their way to England to stay with their brother, a doctor living in Clapham. During the journey my father enjoyed flirting with the two young women whilst I was feeling very sorry for myself as a meal in Kempinski had given me diarrhoea. The meal, consisting of both fish and meat, had been harmless enough but I was not used to eating so much at at once.

*   *   *

Other members of the family took various escape routes out of Russia. Uncle Vitia went south by himself to Turkey and stayed for a while at the Pera Palace Hotel in Istanbul. He was given a few jewels to take with him and I suppose that he lived off the proceeds. He moved first to Germany then to Paris where he survived the wartime occupation. He was helped by the fact that he had a purely Russian surname and did not look at all Jewish. It was not a problem that his patronymic was Jewish and should have appeared on his passport, because so many people had false papers. Uncle Vitia turned up again after the war and told Tante Sophie that he was soon going to be very rich and he would send her some money for Mouma. But he was never seen again because, as always, his business coup failed.

Mouma and Tante Sophie went to Paris where things were very difficult for them. Later, when I was at school in England, I used to send them part of my weekly pocket money. My papa gave me five shillings a week, which was more than necessary. My lunch was paid for on the bill and my only expenses were my fare to school and a doughnut at break. Mother saved some money from housekeeping and this, together with my contribution, was sent to Tante Sophie.

Mouma went to a modest art school and then established herself as a dress designer. She became very successful. In November 1934, the Duke of Kent's bride, Marina, wore a wedding dress which Mouma had designed. Mouma used to sketch at home while other people sold her designs to the

93

fashion houses. The only time she sold direct was to Dmitri Poliakoff, Lazar's playboy son, whose wife had established a haute couture business in Berlin. After Mouma had married, Dmitri arrived at her flat to buy some of her designs while I was staying there. I was however not allowed to see him because she wanted to get through the business as soon as possible. Dmitri fancied himself as a womaniser and Mouma did not want to spend too much time with him.

Mouma made what would have been considered a very successful marriage to Raymond Laporte, a French diplomat whose father was the chairman of the Banque d'Europe Centrale. The Laporte family were staunch Catholics so she converted. Like me, she had been brought up without religion so it did not matter. There was a château in Brittany and a well-appointed flat in the centre of Paris. Although Mouma had already been living fairly well on the profits from her designs, her marriage brought an abrupt change of circumstances.

Mouma and her mother were very close. Mouma's mother-in-law was expected to house Tante Sophie, feed and support her. Before the war Tante Sophie lived in Paris, in a little flat opposite Mouma and her husband. She used to be visited by a Russian chap with a long beard who was obviously quite attached to her. She had a very wide circle of artistic friends and she knew a lot of Russians in Paris so she did not have a bad time. Tante Sophie took it for granted that service would be available wherever she went, regardless of circumstances. She was not shy and she believed that she was meant to be looked after. Thus, we went to quite a superior Russian restaurant in Paris for lunch and she said, "I will not eat anything. I'm not hungry." So we started eating and then she asked, "Well, is it any good? Let's taste it." She continued to sample our food and when she found something she particularly liked she said, "Tell him to wrap some up for me."

Tante Sophie visited us in England in 1960 when she was quite an old lady but, while she was here, she suffered a stroke. She recovered to a certain extent and we found a Caucasian Russian woman to sit with her. But sadly she died in London in our house in Addison Road.

Mouma's husband Raymond, was taken prisoner very soon after the war began and was in a prisoner of war camp in Austria for five years. So Mouma lived with her mother-in-law and her mother in the château in Brittany until a man, who probably bore some grudge against Raymond, started talking about this foreign Jewish woman who was helping to wrap parcels for prisoners of war. So they moved, with false papers, to a remote village in Central France and Mouma did a certain amount of Resistance work. People who knew her in the Resistance used to visit London during the war and bring us messages from her. Then Raymond was liberated and they both came to stay with us for a short period after the war. He was then posted to the French embassy in Warsaw where Mouma died of cancer at the age of thirty-nine. Mouma was strikingly attractive, both in looks and personality, and whenever I met her at Victoria Station, at least three men used to appear carrying her luggage and then they would telephone her and invite her out. She had two daughters; Betka who now lives in Paris and the elder, Catherine, a well known television journalist who like her mother died young of cancer.

*My grandfather's cousin
Lazar Poliakoff in full regalia,
photographed in 1897.*

Lazar Poliakoff in his study, Moscow 1910.

My grandfather's cousin Samuil Poliakoff, the "Railway King of Russia".

Samuil Poliakoff with his son Daniel ca. 1860.

Mouma on her wedding day in Brittany in 1935 wearing a dress of her own design.

My wife, Ina (1913 – 1992).

Martyn, born 1947.

Stephen, born 1952.

Lucinda, born 1957.

Miranda, born 1959.

New emigré; Hyde Park, London 1924.

England

The boat-train from Harwich pulled into Liverpool Street Station fairly early in the morning. We took a taxi to the Savoy Hotel because that was where my father usually stayed when he came to London on business. I was left in the taxi for about twenty minutes while my father went into the hotel. My first sight of London had been very disappointing. What were narrow streets and low buildings beside the gilded onion domes of Russian churches? In Moscow, the traffic had been mostly horse-drawn except for private or government cars. In London, there were hardly any horses, except for those pulling milk delivery carts. Besides, I was used to rather impressive looking cars. Commissar Schmidt had had a Rolls Royce and Commissar Tomski had had the American equivalent, a Pierce Arrow. Father's old car had been a landaulet, like the London taxis of the time, except that his model had a larger bonnet and more lights and horns. I was prevented from making further comparisons of this kind by Father coming out of the Savoy and declaring that the hotel was full. The Wembley Exhibition had just opened and London was over-crowded. So we drove to a block of service flats in Duchess Street, where Father had once stayed for a short period of time.

Duchess Street is just off Portland Place and the block was very near to the Langham Church and the current BBC building. There was a vacant flat on the ground floor with a large reception room and a moderate sized double bedroom but no kitchen. The block was stone-faced and one of the first luxury service flats to be built. It had a restaurant in the basement so that we could be fed in our reception room. The service included a man called William, dressed in green livery with brass buttons. He served our meals, hailed taxis and generally looked after us. After a few days, William said to Father that he could provide flowers for three guineas a week. Father accepted this offer although, of course, we had no money and no immediate prospects of having any. I was thoroughly perturbed by our situation and worried about the future but it did not put my papa off in any way. He was, in many ways, quite a happy individual and extremely self-assured.

While Father was out looking for a job, I used to have my lunch alone with William standing behind my chair. Since we could not communicate, this ritual had to be conducted in complete silence. When we arrived, the full extent of my English was to sing, "It's a long vay to Tipperary, it's a long vay to go," and poor William knew neither Russian nor French. In the evenings, Father and I had nothing to do so Father used to say, "William call a taxi" and we would go out to the cinema, often to see American films. The films were all silent so it did not matter very much that I could not understand

English. After two or three such outings I asked Father, "Do we have to have a taxi every time, why can't we walk?" Clearly it had never occurred to him.

One of the first people to call on us was Dennis, the younger son of Godfrey Isaacs, the Managing Director of Marconi. While in England in 1923, Father had written to us that Dennis had left London and was living in a small town called St John's Wood. Clearly, Father had never been outside the West End except to visit Isaacs in the country. Father showed Dennis the diamond he had brought from Russia and asked him whether he could arrange to sell it, which Dennis did. However it realised only £250, around £7,500 in present day money.

After a few days in England, we were invited to stay with the Isaacs in their country house in Cobham. It was a Regency or early nineteenth century house with forty bedrooms and over a hundred acres. There was a lake where we went fishing, a boathouse, tennis courts and a small golf course. They had a French chef, a butler and two footmen. I was given a room which was meant for a girl, judging from the curtains and bedcover. In the morning there was a knock at the door and a footman came in with a cup of tea and grapes from the greenhouse. I never liked tea and the idea of drinking a cup first thing in the morning seemed singularly unattractive. I did not know what to do, and was looking around the room when I caught sight of the wash-basin so I simply poured the tea away and ate a few grapes. Father had great admiration for Godfrey Isaacs and his wife and they, in turn, appreciated Father's unusual qualities. Godfrey's wife was a Corsican opera singer who claimed that Napoleon was her cousin. They had a grandson called Dickie, younger than me, who died as a boy. We stayed with the Isaacs for a week and I got quite the wrong impression of how people lived in England.

Godfrey Isaacs was the first and long-standing managing director of Marconi. His brother was the Marquis, Lord Reading, who had started off on the Stock Exchange but went bankrupt and decided that being a stockbroker was not a suitable occupation for a gentleman. So he qualified as a barrister and became a very successful King's Counsel. He went on to become a Cabinet Minister, Lord Chief Justice and eventually Viceroy of India. I met him only once. He had striking good looks, although he was by then quite old. Godfrey Isaacs and his two sons were also extremely good looking and athletic. The sons however were spoilt through having too much money and were unable to settle down for very long to any occupation or to any wife. Godfrey Isaacs eventually left Marconi following a row, and died soon afterwards.

Father continued to believe that everything which was English was perfect. However some adjustment was necessary before he was completely at home in the new culture. He thought it incredible when he first saw lovers kissing in public on the grass in the parks in the centre of London. It would have been unheard of in Moscow, quite apart from there being an insufficient supply of grass for the purpose. So he said to his friend Godfrey Isaacs, "What's this? What is going on?" Godfrey Isaacs dryly replied, "A gentleman doesn't look." On another occasion, Father was taken out by Isaacs and his deputy Colonel Simpson, whereupon it was discovered that Father could not fox-trot. He was told to go and learn so he bought himself a pair of dark spectacles because he thought it was not good to be seen taking dancing lessons at his age. The woman who was teaching him kept asking him what was wrong with his eyes.

When I was in my last year at school, my papa decided that I also had to learn to dance. Up to that point, the only tuition I had received had been at the dacha, when for no apparent reason, my Uncle Solomon from St Petersburg had suddenly felt the need to teach his son Vladimir, Mouma and me a series of elaborate dances. One dance, called the *pas d'Espagne,* was very eccentric and to this day I have not met anybody who has heard of it. Then, we danced a polka-mazurka. Clearly this was not very useful when I came West. So my papa took me to tea dances at the Basil Hotel in Knightsbridge. He would say to me, "Why don't you go and ask this one to dance?" and I did what I was told. That is how I started to dance; no formal tuition but gradually getting the right idea. The fashion then was for girls to wear hats like upturned chamber pots which hid their hair. I was dancing with one girl and she asked me the usual question, "Do you prefer blondes or brunettes?" I replied, "Brunettes," upon which she removed her hat to reveal that she was blonde.

At the Isaacs' suggestion, Father went to see Gabbitas Truman & Thring for advice on my education. They did not think Eton the best solution for me and recommended Eastbourne College as the public school to which sons of professional people without much money would go. So away we went to Eastbourne and to this school. The headmaster and housemaster were both horrified to learn that I knew no Latin but seemed much less worried that I knew no English either. They said that I would have to go to a prep school and the housemaster drove us to the one they recommended in an open bull-nosed Morris. Father spoke to the headmaster and it was arranged that I would go there. Fees were seventy-five pounds a term, which I believe was about average for those days.

However, before I could go to the prep school, I had to learn English. Gabbitas Truman & Thring recommended a small establishment in Eastbourne run by a Frenchman, who taught French-speaking boys English. And there I went a few days later, complete with a new bicycle which Father had bought for me in Harrods. The Frenchman was a retired Captain of the Foreign Legion with a waxed moustache and an English wife. She was a typical south coast landlady and could have come from a play by J.B.

Priestley. Her opening conversational gambit was, "What do you think of Pelmanism?" The pupils were housed in a maisonette above a shop in one of the main shopping streets which I believe was called Sussex Gardens. There were only six pupils, including me. One boy came from Nicaragua, had French parents and spoke French as his native tongue and there was an unpleasant boy, a year or so younger than me, who was the son of a provincial shopkeeper. In addition, a young Englishman who worked in a bank, lodged with us.

Instruction in English was given in a small office nearby. The gallant Captain used what he called the 'direct method'. His desk was crowded with small objects which he shunted about saying, "This is near this; this is inside this; this is on top of this" and so on. I made quite good progress in English and learnt to ride my bike. We made daily excursions to the beach and clambered over the rocks working up excellent appetites which we needed in order to force down the English seaside boarding-house food. I remember incredibly sour boiled plums and frizzled up meat. How the gallant Captain suffered it I do not know.

After a comparatively short stay at the school, I was cycling down a hill next to the boy from Nicaragua when our pedals caught and he fell to the right taking my bicycle with him. I fell to the left; my leg was caught in the bicycle frame and the bone in my left thigh snapped. I ended up lying in the road and a small crowd collected around me. I heard a French woman scream in French, "They have killed a French boy." A very primitive Ford ambulance arrived followed by the gallant Captain. I was taken to a nursing home and put into the best room which was enormous. The surgeon diagnosed compound fracture and Father was alerted. He refused to allow an operation in what he termed a provincial hospital and found me a Russian doctor in London. I was taken, this time in a Daimler ambulance, to a nursing home at No. 17 Park Lane, where I stayed for nine months and was operated on twice.

The diamond money must have been running out quite fast. Fortunately the nursing home gave my father credit but when I came out, on crutches, encased in plaster, Father had an unpaid bill for two thousand pounds, about sixty thousand in today's money. I think it took him two or three years to repay this debt. Around this time, Father acquired a male secretary to write his letters in English and research patents in the Patent Office. He was an elderly Englishman called Goodlet who had spent most of his life in Petrograd teaching English in a school. While I was in the nursing home, he was seconded from his work in the Patent Office to teach me English and generally spend some time with me. Although I was initially in considerable pain, I found life in the nursing home quite amusing. I was surrounded by dukes and millionaires' wives. Better still, there was a first-class French chef. Menus arrived twice a day and gave quite a wide choice of extremely well prepared food, a very welcome and very considerable change from Eastbourne!

After my second operation I was put in a room at the back of the nursing home. It was very small indeed with a glass door leading to a fire escape. One day I was in the middle of a lesson with Goodlet when the door burst open and a boy wearing a pyjama top but no trousers rushed through the room. He flung the glass door open, got out onto the fire escape and would have thrown himself off, had Goodlet not caught him by his pyjama top. The boy had just had an appendicitis operation, and had not yet recovered fully from the anaesthetic. The boy's name was Kiryl Fitzlyon Zinoviev; he became a Russian writer and his wife, who is English, is also a writer. Nearly forty years later, I met his wife at Westminster School where our elder son Martyn and their son Sebastian were in the same year.

Before I came out of the nursing home, Father realised that it was not a very good idea living in a service flat in the West End when one was not earning anything. So he took a furnished ground floor and basement maisonette in Elsworthy Road, Primrose Hill, for six pounds a week and engaged a cook-general called Nelly. Several years later Commissar Schmidt came to stay with us in England with Lily, his very smart Jewish wife. When she saw Nelly, who was not unattractive and well-developed in front, serving at the table, she said to Mother, in Russian of course, "If I were you, I would be most worried about having a woman like this in the house." Mother did not respond but I thought it a shocking remark. I was extremely straight-laced and did not react well to blue jokes or that sort of thing.

A Russian Jew, who used to be business manager to Yasha Haifetz, the violinist, was deputed by the Russian Embassy or some other Russian organization to take Schmidt and his wife on a driving tour of England and Scotland. When they returned to London, Schmidt said he had been pleased to see there were some empty spaces in England. He thought England was completely built up.

The house in Elsworthy Road had a pretty garden and good sized rooms and I went there when I came out of the nursing home. It seemed from the furnishings that the owners had spent some time in India. I spent a good deal of my time in a bath-chair but managed to walk about a bit on crutches. The house was divided into two maisonettes. The upper storey was occupied by a retired professor of Physics from the University of Madras called Jones who had a live-in nurse and a cook. The nurse was a pleasant looking, quite plump lady from Glasgow although her family were originally Irish. She looked after me; my leg was still in plaster and I could do very little for myself.

Sir Henry Wood lived in our street and I frequently saw him being driven in a landaulet by a woman. A larger detached house, backing onto Primrose Hill, was occupied by an old lady. Now and again, her entire staff (about ten people in all) would emerge from the house and make her comfortable, with cushions, for a short drive in her car. Opposite us lived the owners of a restaurant in Piccadilly Circus called Monico's. Every morning the family used to set out in large open Fiat: the two sons, the father, mother and an old lady, and every day at midday the old lady used to return bearing a pudding basin which contained her lunch.

While I was convalescing and Mother was still in Russia, Father began to get anxious about my education. The place at the preparatory school in Eastbourne had had to be relinquished and I had missed a lot of schooling. So one morning Father issued out determined to find me a school. He had not walked far along Elsworthy Road before he saw a boy wearing a school cap. He stopped the boy and asked him where he went to school. "To University College School, Hampstead, Sir, " replied the boy.

"Take me there," said my father, and the boy did.

University College School was originally housed in the south wing of the University College building in Gower Street. Early in the century, it had moved into new baroque-style buildings in Frognal, Hampstead. Father marched in, saw the bursar and said, "I have got a clever son. He does not know much English but is getting on. I would like him to come to your school". The bursar said that it would be necessary for me to take the Common Entrance Examination and Father asked him to recommend a tutor. He was given two names; one was Smith and the other Castello. Father came home and said, "What a ridiculous thing, to give me a Spaniard to teach you English". So off he went to see Smith, who was away mountaineering, so Father was forced to go to Castello. The address was Curzon Street. He arrived and rang the bell. The butler said that unfortunately Castello was out but his brother-in-law would see Father. Out came my future father-in-law, Gerald Montagu. Father explained about me and the Common Entrance Examination and enquired whether Castello was a good teacher. Gerald Montagu replied, "He is too good. All his pupils pass their examinations first time, so he hasn't many pupils." Father was impressed by this response and arranged for Castello to visit us since I was not yet mobile. Father had never met Gerald Montagu before; he had, however, met his wife, Firenza, several times, through the Isaacs when he was in England in 1914 and 1916 and had pursued her to some extent. When he returned to Russia in 1916, he brought with him a copy of Tatler in which there were photographs of her. But on this visit to Curzon Street he did not realise that he was talking to her husband.

Castello was duly engaged to teach me, still in French, four or five times a week. He was a very able teacher and an amusing man. He managed to involve himself in both world wars. The second time he was in charge of the camp for Italian prisoners. The Italians gave him a watch as a parting gift and told him, "You were no trouble to us at all."

Castello told his sister about us and after a few lessons, tried to establish whether Father was the man she had met previously. Unfortunately his enquiry took the form of asking me, "Were your people bankers in Russia?" I replied, "Certainly not," because in Communist Russia, bankers were very undesirable relatives. When the banks in Moscow were being closed down, Grandfather's safe in the bank had had to be opened in front of a representative of the family. So my mother went and they cut through the safe and started unloading its contents. There was a large amount of silver and various share certificates (Russian shares were then worth nothing) and some jewellery and they said, "What's all this? How did you get it?" So mother said, "Well my husband is an inventor and he's invented many things." They said, "Well, we like inventors but instead of silver we'll send him away for a holiday in the Crimea." So to be an inventor was respectable but to be in banking, or stockbroking like Grandfather, was terrible. Bankers were blood-sucking capitalists. A few lessons later Castello tried again, asking, "Does your father know a Colonel Simpson?" Simpson was the Deputy Managing Director of Marconi and a friend of Father's. So it was established that we were indeed the right Poliakoffs.

I had no difficulty in passing the Common Entrance Examination and, in the autumn of 1926, became a pupil at University College School. I started my school career on two sticks, then progressed to one and it was only in my third year that I was able to start playing tennis again. Around this time, we left Elsworthy Road and went to live in Park Drive on the borders of Hampstead and Golders Green, near Golders Hill Park. It was a pre-1914, furnished, semi-detached house with five bedrooms, a staircase leading from the kitchen to the maid's bedroom and a small garden. The owners used to be licensees of the Bull and Bush pub in North End Road and there were gold-framed paintings of Highland cattle hanging all over the place.

I was able to walk to the Golders Green Memorial, take the bus and then walk up the hill to school. I was not delivered by car, like some of the other boys, but it soon came to my attention that I had distinguished myself in other ways. There was a boy in my class called Bolsom whose parents had a chain of shoe shops so he knew about shoes. In a History lesson, when we sat on benches not desks, he saw my shoes, seized one and said, "My God, this must have cost at least three guineas." My papa bought all my clothes or had them made and I was always extremely well turned out. I do not think I had stood out at the Russian school where, as far as I remember, I used to wear a Russian shirt because one could not buy anything else, but at University College School I was voted the best-dressed boy in the form.

While Mother was still in Russia, we had very little contact with her as it was not the thing to do to write letters but she was safer once Father had left the country. When she arrived from Russia, a year after us, she was utterly exhausted by having to cope with the death of her father and making all the arrangements for leaving her mother behind in Russia. She had been fortunate in having the help of her half-sisters' children Genia and Boris. Grandmother finally sold the dacha in 1937; she could have come to England but she preferred to go to her elder daughter, Tante Sophie, in Paris and was met by her at the Polish border.

Seeing me on crutches was the final straw for Mother. She had what amounted to a mild nervous breakdown and, for a time, absolutely refused to go out anywhere. My papa took me to the opera a couple of times but generally I think he went out by himself. He never doubted for a moment that people would be delighted to make our acquaintance. No other reaction was possible. Therefore, in England, he continued to mix in upper class circles although we had no money. He made friends with T.P. O'Connor, an Irish Member of Parliament, who was at that time the Father of the House. He became a great friend of Father's and came to rely on him a great deal. At least three nights a week, Father used to go out in white tie to dinner with T.P., as he was known to his friends, and together they went laying foundation stones, opening laundries and so on. I was once taken to tea at his house.

By this time, Father had found a job in the Russian Trade Delegation, which at that time was called Arcos. His salary was ninety pounds a month but Soviet Russians working in London were then treated like diplomats as far as tax was concerned and he was not required to pay any income tax. He was made deputy director of the technical department but he did very little there. His main function was helping the Embassy with protocol, arranging dinners, putting ambassadors in the right places and dealing with visiting delegations from Russia. His many English friends and connections and his knowledge of what the dinner table should look like must have been of considerable help in those early days. He was also earning some money by writing articles for Russian technical journals.

Prompted by me, my papa agreed that perhaps we should think about buying a house. So I went looking around after school and settled on a newly built house in a street in Hampstead Garden Suburb called Middleway. We took out a mortgage and, since the house was unfurnished, Father and I went to Maples and proceeded to buy sheets, pillowcases, cutlery, furniture, everything, including a pseudo-Cromwellian dining room suite and cane furniture for the sitting room.

Meanwhile, Mother soon recovered and had quite a life. She made many friends, not just Russians. Her English was adequate but not brilliant and sometimes she came out with an inappropriate colloquial expression. I was present on one occasion at tea when a guest refused to have another piece of cake and she said to him, "Don't be so cheeky!" The guest was somewhat surprised. Mother never complained about anything and there was no business of, "In Russia we don't do that." She never expected anything and adapted in whatever way was necessary. I used to go to the cinema with my parents, without protest even though I was having to work quite hard at my homework since my English was still poor.

One night in 1929, Father failed to come home for dinner at eight o'clock and there was no telephone call. At eleven thirty, he arrived clearly shaken but pretending to be amused. There had been a police raid on Arcos, and no-one had been allowed to leave. A few days later, it was announced that all the Russians working at Arcos were to be expelled from Britain. It was an unpleasant experience. None of us wanted to go back to Russia and the uncertainty lasted a few weeks. T.P. O'Connor wrote to the Home Secretary, Johnson Hicks, or Jinks as he was known, to say that he could not contemplate life without Father and that he was quite sure that he was totally loyal to Britain and would make a very good citizen. Johnson Hicks replied on a hand-written note saying that he had given instructions that we could live in England without any restriction about employment or anything else. So we were saved.

However, after Arcos was raided, Father was unemployed and did not earn anything to speak of for a couple of years. Things started going very wrong and I decided that we had to sell the house. I was already at college by this time and, while Father was in Paris, I sold it at a profit. We were just in time because the Depression began soon after. For a while it looked as though we had nowhere to go but fortunately my mama had made friends with an old lady in the next cul-de-sac called Miss Robinson who took us in complete with Nelly our maid and we remained there for seven years until I married. By that time, my parents had moved to a flat in New Cavendish Street and they stayed there until the house was sold from under them after the War. Then they came to live in a flat in our house in Albert Place, Kensington, and after that they lived with us in Addison Road.

*   *   *

We knew quite a few Russian emigrés in London. My father worked with Russians in Arcos and knew others from the Embassy but, to begin with, we had relatively little contact with White Russians or the old immigration. There was a club for emigrés in St. John's Wood and I went to a dance there but its membership consisted largely of successful Russian Jews. There was no club for the White Russians apart from the Society of Northern Peoples but at the time I knew nothing of it.

111

My father went to a dinner party given at Lansdowne House by the American millionaire, Gordon Selfridge, who owned Selfridges department store. Selfridge had three daughters; two married viscounts and the third married Prince Vyasemsky. All the daughters and sons-in-law were present at this dinner. Some way through the meal, Prince Vyasemsky said to my papa in Russian, "I must speak to you outside. We can pretend to look at these marble nonsenses." So out they went. He said, "Strictly speaking I am not entitled to call myself Prince Vyasemsky. That was my mother's family but since all the proper heirs are either dead or still in Soviet Russia, I don't think I am doing a great deal of harm, do you?" Father agreed that he was not.

Multitone

In 1931 my father founded Multitone Electric Company, later called Multitone Electronics PLC, with five hundred pounds provided by his solicitor Henry Myer, a splendid chap who had been the youngest colonel in the First World War. He was still very much in touch with his regiment and later used to take me to their annual dances.

I read Physics at University College, London, and joined the fledgling company very soon after I left college in June '31, only a month after Multitone had been registered. Multitone was launched with Father's invention of a superior audio-frequency transformer for radio sets. Father had hired a coil-winding machine and a young woman called Miss Oxley used to come to the house to wind the transformers on Sundays. Clearly the first thing to do was to find premises and I managed to find a place in White Lion Street near the Angel, Islington. It was about fifteen hundred square feet and cost us a hundred and fifty pounds a year, including rates and heating. The premises had to be fitted out and we engaged a carpenter to remove all obstructions and make partitions. On my twenty-first birthday, I was helping the carpenter to get one of the transmission shafts down. He was lowering one end and I was holding the other when, being oily, it slipped from his hand and fell on my foot. It felt as if my foot had been smashed to bits so I sent the carpenter out to get a taxi while I looked up a doctor's address. Then, the carpenter fetched me a large whisky from a nearby pub and we set out for the surgery. The doctor told me that I had not broken anything, gave me a bottle of something to dull the pain and sent me home in the taxi. When I arrived, there was a little tea party in honour of my birthday but unfortunately it was not a particularly enjoyable occasion for me.

The Multitone premises were divided into an office for my papa, a factory for the girls yet to be engaged and a lab for me. Soon we had taken on quite a few girls, starting with a Miss Haynes, and began making transformers. For my part, I designed a piece of equipment to test the windings.

In those days, people used to build their own radio sets. Every week or month magazines such as "Practical Wireless" and "Wireless World" would have instructions for building a set called "The Magic Five" or some such name and would specify the components needed to build it. Generally, the magazine would not make exclusive recommendations but would suggest more than one possible supplier. Clearly, the thing to do was to get into "The Magic Five." By that time, I had designed a tone control transformer which when used with a potentiometer, brought the audio-response curve from high pitched to level to low pitched. Up till then, you could cut the treble but to rock the response curve by rotating a single knob was quite unprecedented. So that was our way into almost exclusive specification for the audio frequency transformers for these sets.

We could not however interest radio manufacturers in our tone control transformer until my papa met the senior manager of a cigarette firm over dinner. They made a brand called Kensitas which in those days had quite a large factory near Old Street. At the time, they were busy giving away radio sets in return for coupons on their cigarette packets. The main manufacturers refused to make the coupon sets because they competed with the normal retail trade. So Kensitas used an unknown manufacturer functioning on quite a large scale making a thousand sets a week. My father told the Kensitas manager that it was totally unrealistic to expect people to want the coupon sets without a tone control transformer. So the manager agreed to fit our transformers to his radios. I went to see the manufacturers of the coupon sets, Corey Parsons. Corey had been a superior tailor in Moscow and knew nothing about sets at all but Parsons was quite knowledgeable. We secured the order and from then on we worked overtime making a thousand transformers per week for these sets.

That was in '33 and meanwhile a number of technical developments had occurred. Radio sets in those days were almost all battery operated which meant that you had an accumulator which had to be recharged as well as a high tension battery of 120 volts or so. The amount of current used was very considerable and two systems came along which reduced the drain on the battery. One of these, called Class B, prevented the valve from passing any current unless there was a signal; when the signal did come, the high tension current would increase and follow the sound wave. Fortuitously, I came across someone demonstrating Class B at the Physical Society Exhibition and as a result we were able to come out with the necessary transformers and chokes for the constructor market before anybody else did. I also managed to persuade Marconi, and Mullard which belonged to Philips, to contribute articles for a little booklet called "The Multitone Guide to 'Push-Push' Amplification." Everyone in Multitone helped to post them and that year our trade blossomed. We continued to work overtime and made our first profit.

Around this time, a wireless set manufacturer went bankrupt and its entire staff arrived on our doorstep. Some of these manufacturers were professional bankrupts who were really engaging in fraud. They would order a lot of materials and start making and selling radio sets. The sales would not go very well because nobody had heard of them and so they would go bankrupt. Part of the stock would be removed at night before anybody noticed, and the rest was bought by somebody else through the liquidator. In a week or so, a new company that had already been registered would be in business making sets. I think one company called Ionic went bankrupt nine times.

My father had been experimenting with powerful thermionic hearing aids, instead of the usual mechanical hearing aids. The hearing aid business used to be a very dirty trade and deaf people were constantly being swindled. My papa visited Ear, Nose and Throat specialists who were extremely impressed both by the apparatus and by him and started sending patients to us. We opened consulting rooms in New Cavendish Street, on the corner of Portland Place. We had quite a few people working there; two secretaries, four consultants, a butler who opened the door and a repair team in the basement. My papa was there all the time, seeing people himself and supervising the other consultants. Patients came both independently and accompanied by a specialist. We never sold anything outright but let people try the hearing aids on approval. Unless they were totally deaf, this never failed.

One day a man wearing a grey tailcoat and top hat rushed in and demanded to see Father. When he was told that Mr Poliakoff was seeing someone, he said, "I am Sir Spencer Marion Wilson, Lord of the Manor of Hampstead. I am not used to waiting." After a while he was let in and they shook hands. He said, "I've shot nine hundred and sixty-three stags and by Jove before I'm gone, I'll shoot the thousandth". Then he had a hearing aid trial and heard very well. So he took a hearing aid away with him and died many years later without ever having paid for it. There was quite a correspondence because he objected to the battery lasting only six months. The first time our manager wrote to him he addressed the letter "Dear Sir", instead of "Sir" as he should have done and received a printed card saying that as a baronet of so many years antiquity he expected to be correctly addressed. After a month or two another mistake was made and a similar card arrived on the top of which was printed SECOND WARNING.

My parents lived above the consulting rooms at New Cavendish Street and I frequently went to lunch there. Sometimes on my visits, they were short staffed in the consulting rooms and I would see a deaf person. Quite a few patients came from abroad and, on one occasion, a very heavily built woman came with a tiny husband who was deaf. They were Sassoons from Alexandria or Cairo. So I fitted the hearing aid and we sat down. The woman said in French, "Look at him, the poor man. He can't hear at the opera; he can't hear what I say; he goes to the Stock Exchange and he can't hear. I think sometimes it would be better for him to be dead." When he heard that he jumped. So she said, "You heard that?"

He said, "Of course I heard it".

She declared, "A miracle!"

Some patients became very attached to my papa and pheasants and salmon used to rain on him in their season. When he visited the Princess Royal to supervise the fitting of a hearing aid, he was asked to dinner and to stay the night. She was married to Lord Lascelles and their estate was somewhere not far from Leeds. Father entertained them by playing Russian songs on the piano which they professed to appreciate. After my father died, I went with an assistant to see her in St James's Palace on two or three occasions. The Princess was very nice and we talked about Fabergé. One of these visits was scheduled just before she was due to go to a royal garden party. She was given a new style of hearing aid which fitted behind the ear and then the Princess, her lady-in-waiting and I went out into the garden for a rehearsal. I had to pretend to be different people and as I approached, her lady-in-waiting would say, "The Mayor of Portsmouth" very quietly to make sure she could hear. When we had done this for a while, the Princess said, "Is this thing going to stay on?" Then she jumped very high into the air and landed heavily to find out.

Father's star turn however, was Winston Churchill. A baronet closely allied with Conservative Central Office purchased one of our hearing aids and was very impressed with it so he arranged for my papa and his assistant to visit Downing Street. After that, they used to revisit Churchill from time to time to make sure his several hearing aids were working and I have a letter from Churchill thanking Father for his care. If the appointment was in the morning, they would find Churchill in bed sniffing at a glass of whisky. On one occasion, Father's assistant brought one of Churchill's books with him which he asked Churchill to sign. Churchill obliged and then said with a grin, "I've written others as well you know."

There is an unfortunate property of the middle ear; low and middle notes start masking high notes as the volume of sound is increased. This is true for all people, not just for the deaf. But it is the deaf that are caught. The deaf person requires a certain amount of amplification but when this is given, he or she cannot hear the high notes and so cannot distinguish 's' from 'f' and so on. Therefore I started insisting that, whenever possible, people should use both ears. Then we could feed only the high notes into one ear. Since there is no masking between one ear and the other, we could give a considerable volume in one ear while still retaining the appreciation of high notes through the other. I called this "unmasked hearing" and in everything we did, we tried to make people use both ears.

We manufactured a special wireless set for the deaf which consisted of a normal, portable, battery-operated set to which the family could listen in the usual way, while the deaf person had an extension lead with armchair volume control and earphones. However, if instead of listening to the radio, the deaf person wanted to listen to the conversation in the room, at the turn of a switch it became the most powerful hearing aid of its time. We exhibited it at Radio Olympia and journalists were invited for a preview on the day before the exhibition officially opened. There was nothing interesting for them to write about except for our set so we had excellent advance publicity. The next day, a long queue formed at our stand with deaf children, old people and so forth wanting to try our set. To begin with I was alone on the stand and, for the whole week of the show, there were immensely dramatic scenes. There was generally an audience about six deep outside the stand and people were brought in to try the set one at a time. In many cases, there were brilliant results, colossal excitement and sometimes tears. That, of course, launched us into serious hearing aid work which we were rather slow to follow up but eventually, in addition to the set, we launched a "portable" hearing aid which weighed seven and a half pounds, had an accumulator and a high tension battery of sixty volts and, most importantly, a crystal microphone. We had to persuade people that they could carry around such a large piece of equipment but they heard wonderfully with it and we did very well, spreading our gospel of high-quality hearing aids. We went on making our hearing aids in a small way during the war, although we had great difficulty in getting batteries.

For a long time Siemens bought our hearing aids and sold them through their own channels. Their medical side, Siemens Reiniger, was based just outside Nuremburg. I went there with a battery supplier to see Peter von Siemens. It was just after the war and there was very little left of Nuremburg, but we stayed in a reasonably watertight hotel. On the first night, von Siemens took me out to dinner in a Bavarian village and the following night, the battery supplier and I were left to our own devices. We did not know what to do, so we hailed a carriage with a pair of white horses and drove round the ruins of Nuremburg. My companion said quite wittily that we should be photographed, he and I, on our export drive.

To begin with, I designed almost every new product that came out. Then I had first one assistant and eventually two. In '37 my father very nearly died from emphysema and I became Managing Director of what was still a fairly small company employing only fifty people. After that I no longer had time to design new products myself.

In '39 I met a brigadier at a charity luncheon in aid of the Margate School for the Deaf. It seemed that war was imminent so I said that I was keen to get involved. He arranged for me to go to the Horse Guards and talk to a major and I volunteered for commission in signals. The major received me with the enthusiasm of a maître d'hôtel. I filled in a form and went on holiday to the South of France. Before we left, I received a letter forwarded by a general saying that I was accepted but would I please give my naturalisation number. Not realising that it was on my passport, I thought I would let him know when I got back. Then we were delayed for a week because Ina, my wife, was poisoned by mushrooms in Nevers and it was not until a few days after my return to England that I wrote away with my naturalisation number. Eventually I received a letter from the general saying, what a pity, but unfortunately the recruitment was already complete. So that was how I missed the war.

The company clearly needed to have war work or our staff would have been sent elsewhere. Fortunately we were introduced to the radio manufacturer Cossor, the first to make radars. We became the principal mechanical sub-contractor, machining parts out of solid blocks of plastic for fast developing radar systems because there was no time to make mouldings. We worked long hours, acquired more machine tools and began to need more space. There were three or four buildings adjacent to the building in which we already occupied two floors. We finished by occupying all of them. We began to receive contracts direct from the Admiralty to make all sorts of elaborate electronic units and thus became an Admiralty firm. Ultimately, we manufactured complete radars. These went to Russia and had to be sent to an X-ray firm to be engraved with Cyrillic lettering.

By this time, we had a very wide range of products. Mostly, we manufactured things that the technical divisions of the Admiralty, Air Force or Army had cooked up but we also had a few designs of our own. The most notable of these was something we called Telesonic, a system of one-way voice transmission which did not use radio and was originally designed for hearing aids in theatres and cinemas. A loop of wire was laid down and the audio signal was fed directly into it. The deaf person had a box in which there was a three valve amplifier and a coil which picked up the signal from the loop. This gave perfect hearing and allowed the deaf person to sit anywhere in the cinema. Two theatres owned by a father and son stood back to back, the Wyndham and the New (now the Albany). Our Telesonic design was imitated by another hearing aid manufacturer, Amplivox, and they got to the New Theatre before we did but we supplied Wyndhams. Because the theatres were back to back, people using hearing aids could sometimes hear what was going on in the other theatre. In the middle of one performance at the New Theatre, all the deaf people suddenly stood up. The performance at Wyndhams had finished and they were playing God Save. We adapted these inductive hearing aids for bridging companies which worked at night, putting up pontoon bridges, and which were not allowed to use radio because it would give away their position. It was very successful and we got a contract from every bridging company there was.

Another of our designs was the Bomb Clock Detector for Air Force bomb disposal squads. The original German time bombs had a clock which ticked away; when the clock stopped, the bomb would explode. Our detector consisted of a substantial box, worn like a satchel over the body, headphones, a crystal microphone and a magnet which clamped on to the bomb. With our equipment, the disposal team could listen to the clock and the moment it stopped they would run like hell.

We had a large air raid shelter under our main building in St John Street, which had been requisitioned for us by the Ministry of Aircraft Production, and when the Blitz was at its height, several families who had been made homeless used to stay there at night. I told people during the Blitz that I was not at all impressed by the bombs because during the October Revolution, we had withstood an artillery barrage for a whole week with no let-up at all. I lived in my office a for few nights every week and the rest of the time I stayed overnight with Ina and my in-laws in a hotel in the country. During this period, my drill at Multitone was quite taxing. Breakfast would be brought to my office from the canteen. Then I would go to the gate to encourage the chaps coming in. I functioned in the ordinary way for the rest of the day and would go out to dinner but returned to see the night-shift in. After that I would walk round the shelter. I went to bed at one o'clock and rose again at seven and so it went on.

Probably, our most fraught project for the Ministry of Supply was manufacturing the radio transmitters which were dropped by parachute. They were designed partly by the Ministry and partly by us and were used for all airborne landings, including the unfortunate Arnhem affair. Soon after we began manufacturing them, the Ministry started getting very anxious and said we had to move the contract out of London. We could not understand why; the Blitz was substantially over, so what was all the excitement? Well, we soon found out that it was because of the flying bombs. So I rushed around looking for a country house with enough room to house all the girls and to make the transmitters but I could not find anything suitable. The Ministry meanwhile got used to being threatened by flying bombs. We never got hit, although a chap across the road was killed while he was in his bath.

We expanded from fifty employees to seven hundred, including one hundred and fifty people working in the machine shop and fourteen people in the tool room. After the war, we wanted to keep on as many of these people as possible so we rushed into a hotchpotch of manufacturing projects. We made a hundred operating tables about half of which were sent to Russia by Lady Churchill's fund. We made anaesthetic equipment which, at the time, was the most advanced on the market. We formed a company with a man named Blise, who had designed the anaesthetic equipment, manufacturing inhalers for pregnant women. We made radio sets for export in metal cases for hot climates, all-purpose amplifiers, electric-convulsant apparatus to cure people of undesirable ideas by giving them electric shocks through their heads and electro-medical diagnostic and treatment units for departments of physical medicine. We had no experience of costing these products and the quality of plating we gave our syringes, for example, was altogether excessive. Almost all our new products lost money and we had to cut down from employing several hundred people to employing just over a hundred.

When it came to making redundancies, I addressed the work force in two groups. I was obviously so upset that they could not be angry.

Our accountant, Cooper, lost his head when he saw our accounts and, without my knowledge, wrote to our chairman Henry Myer saying that he thought we were bankrupt. I received a very bitter letter from Myer who said that he had told our bank, Coutts, that they should call in a receiver. I had no option but to deal with the situation head on. First of all, I had Cooper in and we went through the grounds on which he had written to our chairman. He admitted that we were not bankrupt and agreed to write a letter of retraction to Myer, saying that he had overreacted. After that, I took myself off to Coutts, calmed their fears and then went to see another director named Hill, or Hilly Billy as I called him. He telephoned Myer and reiterated that there was no need for the company to go bankrupt. Coutts appointed a senior accountant and an assistant to supervise us. Nervo and Nox, as I called them after the comedians of the time, decided that we ought to have a moratorium. A large meeting was held in a colossal hall and Nervo made a speech saying that Multitone's difficulties were only temporary. He announced that the February sales were very good and said, "Think of such sales in February, the worst possible month." There was a general air of prosperity in the country and our new products were well received, so we had been successful in sales although not in profits. Everyone agreed with Nervo and a committee was appointed to take an interest in what we were doing. The only dissenter was the gas company to which we could not have owed very much because we did not use gas for industrial processes. All of the others turned on the unfortunate representative of the gas company and shouted at him until he eventually signed.

We were in moratorium for quite a time but it was not a particularly anxious period. Although we were paying out continually, I was selling everything that could be sold. First of all we sold the lease of our premises to the owners of Vogue. We continued to occupy the top floor until we moved to our present premises in Underwood Street several years later where we began with only two buildings, belonging to the cigarette company Rothmans, and expanded from there. We had purchased an excess of raw materials for our new products, brass for syringes, magnets for bone conductors, enamelled wire and so on and, since there was a shortage of raw materials, I was able to sell such things very well. I sold my father's limousine and my own car but at the same time we ordered some cars for our salesmen so for a while I used one of those, a Hillman Minx. I think we began our moratorium by owing something like a hundred thousand pounds, about two million in today's money, so it took us some time to pay our debts. Our first payment was one pound two shillings. But business picked up all the time. Really our most important decision was to stick it out and face everybody. All this happened very soon after our elder son Martyn was born in '47 and we were clear of it about three years later.

We started making translation equipment for exhibitions, conferences and so on. We supplied Woburn Abbey, amongst other places. Visitors would pick up one of our machines, the Lorgnette, as they went in, choose one of four languages and be guided through the Abbey. The owners wanted to get people in and out as quickly as possible so the recording chased you round, "This is whatever painting, it was painted in whatever year" and then straight on to the next one. Our first conference was the biggest post-war conference in London. It was held in the Albert Hall and was on the subject of artificial fibres. We supplied several thousand Lorgnettes and the man in charge of the contract at Multitone left before the conference began in case the Lorgnettes failed to work. Eventually, we set up a subsidiary company, which we later sold off, to manufacture this equipment. For a while, we had some competition but that perished and then the Germans designed a very neat machine, an improvement on our Lorgnette, directed by infra-red heat that is pulsated and picked up at different frequencies. But our translation equipment still works and is regularly booked for conferences.

We acquired a speciality in diagnostic electronic units for departments of Physical Medicine. Our equipment determined how many volts had to be applied to a muscle to make it work and from that the doctors could diagnose what was wrong. We did very well with these; the Ministry of Health bought fifty and distributed them to hospitals as essential equipment and we had people going round hospitals recommending them. One day our principal salesman, who was a physiotherapist himself, walked into St. Thomas's Hospital, London, and found that they were trying to make a paging system. They had installed an enormous amplifier with a loop aerial which effectively prevented anyone talking on the telephone because the signal broke through. In fact, hardly any electrical instrument could function in such a high field and people with hearing aids riding on buses outside the hospital suddenly found that they were being yelled at. So, in 1956, St Thomas's asked us to make them a paging system which we did in about six months. After they had used it for a month, they gave a demonstration to the BBC and press. We got a colossal amount of publicity but it was still very hard to interest even hospitals. So we started to carry out work studies, measuring the average time it took switchboards to find people. In the case of Hammersmith Hospital, this turned out to be five minutes. We would say, "Here are the results. We will now install our system free of charge. Then we'll do the same survey and you will see how much less time it takes." With the pagers, it took seconds rather than minutes and we never lost a sale. There was considerable overseas interest in our pagers. We even supplied our system to the Kremlin Hospital, where I used to toboggan as a child.

We gave a dinner dance at the Savoy Hotel for our twenty-fifth anniversary celebrations, a year late in '57 instead of '56. The Director of Signals, General Butler, with whom I had worked during the war, travelled specially from Ireland to be with us and he made an excellent speech. Our new Dutch agent sent a cable that said, "The Channel divides us but fifty one channels unite us" because at the time the pagers had fifty one channels. Of course, you cannot run any business now without pagers but the idea did not catch on immediately. There were some exceptional, forward-looking companies. ICI, for example, was an early customer. But the motor industry and hotels were slow to adopt electronic paging.

I was not brought up in a commercial culture. Essentially I am, in a small way, an industrialist, a maker of things and an innovator. I have always tried to be a good employer, to make people feel that they were valued and part of the team. So there is a great deal of loyalty to the company and it is a pleasant place to work. But worrying whether the laminations cost whatever they cost or sixpence more was never something I found very thrilling. Had there been no Revolution, I would have been sent to Cambridge, as my papa had planned, and presumably I would have had to spend a year or more in England to learn English properly. It is difficult to imagine what I would have done having finished Cambridge but earning a living would not have been a high priority.

When I ceased to be chairman of Multitone at the age of sixty-seven, I was nominated for an O.B.E. for exports. Seventy percent of Multitone's production was exported. This was achieved through effort and through having products of sufficient novelty to be readily marketable. Ina and our two daughters accompanied me to the Palace and we were coached as to the proper form of address, how to walk and how low to bow. We talked amongst ourselves and then we filed, in the order the authorities thought best, to receive our Honours. The Queen congratulated each person and asked what their Honour was for. We were photographed outside the Palace, and then the car took us off to lunch at Ma Cuisine in Walton Street, all dressed up.

The electronics field has changed beyond recognition since I first started in business. All the companies which we considered colossal and safe, and all of the component manufacturers that supplied us, have gone. Ferranti manufactured turbines and dynamos for power generation in Manchester. They made a radio set transformer that was built like a battleship and, whereas our transformer cost seventeen and sixpence, theirs cost thirty five shillings and occupied three times as much space. When they were in full health, they employed twenty-three thousand people. Then there was Plessey, founded by a German tool designer called Heine, changed to Hein, and an American, Alan Clark who became a British subject and was knighted. They were the first mass-producers in electronics.

At that time, Marconi were making a radio set called "the straight eight", an enormous box with eight dials. You walked along and tuned to the station you required by turning one dial after another. It was made by instrument makers, who wore steel spectacles and white aprons. They made everything from first principles except for the cabinet: the mahogany chassis, the cut-out, the turnings, so you can imagine how long it took. Alan Clark went to see Godfrey Isaacs, the Managing Director of Marconi and said, "I don't care what this thing costs you. I'll make it for ten percent less" and he got an order. But he had nothing except ideas so he came back and said, "I'd be very grateful if you could make me an advance to buy a plant." That is how Plessey started and they spread right through the radio field, making components. Their technical salesman used to come in and say, "Who are you getting this from? We'll make it for ten percent less." They grew continuously and during the war, the factory in Ilford spread underground and they had plants all over the place. They continued to do well after the war but when Alan Clark died, his two sons took over and they were not such successful managers. Plessey was broken up. Part went to GEC and part went to Siemens. So it disappeared.

Multitone is in the business of electronics, an area dominated by multinationals many times its size but it has flourished in this environment by developing a niche. The multinationals are handicapped because they want to to have a finger in every electronic pie. Multitone has now been taken over by the Hong Kong based telepaging group, Champion Technology. People ask me whether I feel sad about this but my answer is "Absolutely not". The main thing, having spent all my working life in the company, is for it to flourish, for its name to continue to be held in high esteem and for employment to increase.

My parents

I was recently introduced to the Russian chess grand master, David Bronstein, who kept asking me, in Russian, "How did your family manage to survive for seven years under the Regime?" The answer, I believe, lies in my father's character. The authorities needed scientists and Father, whose confidence in himself was absolute, was able to persuade them that his potential must be protected. The years were characterised by danger and frustration. We were threatened by lawless brigands and eviction by the authorities. But my father was one of those rare individuals who are really not afraid of anything. And it was this refusal to be intimidated, combined with his tremendous energy and determination, that carried us safely through the post-Revolutionary period.

Father was always promoting some new idea or invention. In post-Revolutionary Russia, the night trains from Moscow were lit only by candle lanterns above the doors. This was obviously very unsatisfactory and Father decided that it would not be too difficult to manufacture small dynamos, which could power lights like the bicycle lamps which are activated by pedalling. It was not easy to couple dynamos to the carriage wheels in Russia so soon after the Revolution, so Father decided that the passengers would turn handles to provide the electricity. He made drawings and, in my presence, discussed the idea with the Commissar of Labour. He said, "These people are spending their time in idle chatter. Why can't they do something useful and turn the handles to light the carriage so that other people can read or write?" Schmidt appeared to take Father quite seriously but it was not made clear how volunteers for this socially useful work would be recruited.

In England, Father thought of a way to make long playing records. The problem which had to be solved was that the speed of the record relative to the needle becomes slower and slower as the needle goes towards the centre. Before modern long playing records were invented, Father had the brilliant idea of driving the record with a drive wheel underneath so that no matter where the needle was, the speed relative to the groove would be constant. This meant you could have a much longer recording, without having to record the tracks on the inside and outside of the record at different speeds. I was much struck by this idea and wrote a little prospectus for it.

During the war, Father thought of degaussing ships, as far as I am aware, before anyone else did. The ship's metal mass triggered off magnetic mines as it passed. Father's idea was to put a loop around the ship, with a substantial current going through it, to neutralise the ship's magnetism. He talked to the Admiralty and then I think they started degaussing the ships themselves.

Father was an inventor, not a business man. He was in some ways touchingly unsophisticated as far as money was concerned and costs did not interest him at all. I was not particularly business minded but, in comparison with him, I was a Rothschild and after a while he let me guide him quite a bit. He was not an easy man but very lovable and our relationship was exceptionally close.

My parents lived for many years above our consulting rooms in New Cavendish Street where there was a lift that went up to their front door. The flat itself was on three floors but they never had any problems going up the internal staircase as they were lightly built. One wintry Sunday afternoon when there was snow on the ground, my parents decided to go for a walk. On their return, they got into the lift which was a typical small, medical district lift but it stopped. My papa took out his pocket screwdriver, unscrewed the mahogany panels and at the age of nearly seventy, squeezed through the opening, climbed over an extensive gap into the flat, brought down a ladder and fished my mother out. They were so electrified by this experience that they felt they'd had a holiday. I would have given in and thought "to hell with it, wait till Monday." But my papa was a very unusual character.

Whatever Father did, he did perfectly. He had the gift of absolute concentration and once he decided to do something, no trouble seemed too much. He took the view that every problem has a solution and he was very good about looking forward rather than back. He was musically gifted, played the piano very well and sometimes composed. He also painted and, in his old age, he liked colouring prints which destroyed their value but it did not matter. Father never retired but went to work up to two days of his death at the age of eighty-seven. He continued with his efforts for the deaf, visiting deaf schools and trying to discover how much the children heard and to what extent it was possible to give them conversational hearing.

My mother exercised enormous influence behind the scenes, although always overshadowed by Father's charismatic personality. Father believed in his inventions with an almost religious fervour and showed terrific determination to realise his ideas as quickly as possible. He was not worried by things going wrong if he could put them right. But he lacked my mother's stamina. In her quiet way, she was a much stronger character and was able to help him over many difficult times. Mother was extremely controlled and never said anything to upset my father. He told her everything and she was a wonderful support to him. When he said everything was a disaster, she would say no, it is for the best, it will all come right. They had a very successful marriage. I do not think for a moment that my papa was consistently faithful but they cared for each other very much and it worked.

Father was forever telling us about his ideas but, although Mother listened, I do not think she ever tried to understand his inventions. She was well read. She spoke perfect French and good German, having lived in Germany when she was first married. Just before the Revolution, she was also taking English lessons. But she was no blue-stocking and her main interest was in people.

My mother died in our house in her ninety-seventh year. Throughout her life, she showed a great concern for all sorts of humble people. In England, of course, we had very little money but nevertheless we always kept staff and they were very devoted to her. She used to go to the little shops off Addison Road to buy odds and ends and was greatly loved by every small shopkeeper, every delivery boy and milkman. She listened attentively to their troubles and when necessary helped them with money. Often they continued to keep in contact with her until they died.

Return to Russia

The first time I went back to Russia was for the British Exhibition in '66. I flew, while Ina and our son, Martyn, went by train and I arrived first. We had been allocated rooms in the Aeroflot Hotel near the old airport but, when I arrived at the hotel, I was told that they had not received our booking and that they were full. For the moment, there was nothing I could do, so I sat on a bench and talked to an old Jewish woman until Martyn and Ina arrived in a car and said we had been put into a hotel called Ostankino. It was unspeakably awful; the bedrooms were basic beyond words and the shower, as I complained to the Intourist people, was only suitable for washing down cows. The only redeeming feature was the half-French girl called Veronique in the Service Department who was very helpful. She told us that the restaurant was dreadful but we should ask for Anna and say that Veronique had sent us. I did as she suggested and Anna marched up to table where a man was sitting and said, "Get out of here". Anna looked after us very well but the restaurant was full of Scottish workmen who were setting up the exhibition and who drank too much vodka and fought. Their manager was an ex-ballet-dancer and was quite incapable of controlling them. After three days, we talked our way into a much better hotel.

The exhibition was held in Sokolniki Park, just outside Moscow where there were more than twenty exhibition pavilions, a park and a lake. Multitone had a corner of the AEI stand because we were working with them to supply pagers for coal mines. AEI (Associated Electrical Industries) was a large company later taken over by GEC. Before the exhibition opened, I was checking that all was well when we were told that the First Deputy to the Minister of Foreign Trade wanted to be shown round. The AEI manager of the stand said, "The stand's not ready. I'm going" so he beat it and I was left with his assistant and my son Martyn who had come to work at the exhibition before going up to Cambridge. The Minister arrived with an entourage of twenty people and the assistant from AEI started to show them models of dynamos of so many megawatts. But whatever they were shown, the Minister said Russia had bigger and better.

Suddenly, I recognised Khrianin, an old friend from the Trade Delegation in London, in the Minister's entourage. Khrianin pointed to one of our exhibits and told the Minister, "There is something interesting over there." The exhibition did not yet have any electricity but Martyn said to me, "I'll press the key and you press the self-bleeper" which was an adequate demonstration in the circumstances. The Minister said, "That's quite interesting. May I have the literature?"

When the exhibition opened, a chap appeared and said to me in Russian, "I would like to speak to Mr Poliakoff, Chairman of Multitone AEI." I demoted myself, explaining that I was only chairman of Multitone and he said that Pavlenko, the Director of the Exhibition, wished to invite me to a meeting the next day. At the meeting, there were six or more people. When Pavlenko came to introduce me to one man, responsible for some technical area, he said he was a prince, and in case I misunderstood repeated, "a marquis."

Pavlenko said that if we lent him our equipment for use at the next exhibition, he would give us a discount on a stand. As a result the whole Sokolniki Park was covered by our system and we finished up with two stands: the one we had paid for, and another spanning a bridge which connected two pavilions. Pavlenko brought every minister to see us. He used to wait until they were approaching the stand and then he would say into his transmitter, "Ivan Nikolaevich, tell Comrade such-and-such about these machines" and Ivan Nikolaevich would do so via the pager. When Brezhnev came, the exhibition was closed for his visit. It was raining and crowds were getting wet, waiting outside. He was much shorter than I had realised. We shook hands and exchanged the usual Russian greetings. We started to give the demonstration but a tall man, who turned out to be the Minister for Instrument Construction, broke in and said, "Superficially, this is a very attractive system but it is very dear and we are working on one ourselves." Brezhnev looked displeased but Pavlenko did not lose his composure and said, "Nonsense, Alexander Iosifovitch will give you a discount."

A few years later, at another exhibition, I was in our office with our friend Khrianin. He was tucking into caviar sandwiches and drinking whisky and brandy when one of the helpers rushed in and said the Minister of Instrument Construction was at our stand. So I came out and greeted the Minister. He said, "Well now, I would like a system for my ministry and for our house of rest. You give me a nice discount and I will buy." (Houses of rest were large seaside or country houses owned by Ministries and industries for their employees to go to for holidays.) Later his assistant appeared carrying a box and said, "This is a clock to time chess moves. Throw the box away. I don't think you'll like the smell. It's the glue."

On our first visit to Russia, a woman came to the stand and said, "You have no idea what terrible things are happening here. I want to meet you outside the gates of the park." She was obviously an agent provocateur so I alerted the young people on the stand, who were all students or recent graduates, and said I was going to have nothing to do with her. When she returned I said, "I'm sorry. We are foreigners here. We can't possibly take any part in anything that is going on."

Many of the Soviet Russians I met when I started going back were aggressively communist but their enthusiasm cooled every year. In Sochi, we met a woman on the beach. It was still quite cold and she said to me, "Of course you have to keep healthy in England because it costs so much to be ill". I said, "No, no it's free. There is the National Health Service" but she said, "That's not what they tell us" and refused to believe me.

One weekend, we drove with Mouma's younger daughter, Betka and her godmother, Juliette, to the famous monastery town of Zagorsk where we had taken refuge for a short period after the October Revolution. Juliette was French but was married to the Swiss Ambassador in Moscow. As we passed the signs for Mamontovka I said, "That was where we had our dacha" and they insisted that we go and look. I had some difficulty in deciding that it was indeed our dacha. The trees had grown and the dacha itself was unpainted and derelict. We walked into the grounds and an old man looked out of a window. I said to him, like Goldilocks and the three bears, "I used to live here as a boy and what is more you are sitting on one of our chairs!" He rushed out on to the east-facing terrace and asked, "Is Emma Nikolaevna still alive?" This shook me and left me speechless for some moments. Apparently, my grandmother had sold the house to a government organization who had put six families in there, thirty people in all. The top of the dacha had been made habitable in winter but all the service buildings had disappeared. The man I spoke to had only one room for all his family. They were very kind and told me to come again.

Another year, I was in Russia, again for the British Exhibition, and nothing much was happening so I said to my driver, "To hell with it. I'll go and see my dacha again." This time I met not only the couple from my previous visit but also their daughter, son-in-law and small grandchild. It was five o'clock and they were just sitting down to lunch because they had been picking mushrooms. My driver and I had already eaten but no amount of protestation prevented us from having to eat another lunch of *lapsha* (vermicelli soup) and *pojarski* cutlets washed down with cherry brandy. My third visit was with Ina, our son Martyn and his wife Janet in 1970. The dacha had been demolished. I found that extremely upsetting and was out of spirits for the rest of the day. Martyn collected some marigold seeds from the garden as a remembrance. They were going to build a house of rest on the site but I do not suppose it has been built yet.

We had some difficulty in locating my cousin Genia in '66 but eventually succeeded. She was the daughter of Milia, my mother's half-sister and the youngest of Grandfather Shabbat's children from his first marriage. Genia was a good deal older than me, Nordic looking with flaxen hair and blue eyes, slightly plump but very pleasant to look at. She was an artist and we used to see her often, particularly in the country. Our next-door neighbour

Sarafanov's nephew, Ivan Ivanovitch had become very keen on her and used to seek her company whenever she came. She was an extraordinarily kind and caring person and she was a great help before my mama left. She visited our grandfather when he was dying, organized a Jewish funeral for him and made a sketch for the memorial stone.

When I went back to Russia, for the first time in forty-two years, she was still living in the flat where she had been born. Her father's name was still fixed to the door, although he had been dead for thirty years. Genia went to an art college and then drew propaganda posters on commission to encourage Russians to produce more or to be encouraged that they had already produced more. I remember seeing her hanging her latest creation on the wall when I was staying with her family on first going to school in Moscow. It had graphs and a picture of potatoes. Genia then went to the Sculpture Institute where she met her husband, the sculptor Vilenski, who came from Vinitza in the Ukraine. His father, an Orthodox Jew, wore a skullcap and made barrels. One would not expect a boy from this background to become an artist but he was very gifted. He became the number one sculptor in Russia even though he was not a Party member. By Russian standards, his art was reasonably unconventional but it was very traditional by Western standards. He was quite Jewish. I told them that Martyn and I had visited the Moscow synagogue and he said to Genia, "Why don't we go to the synagogue?" to which she replied, "Don't talk nonsense."

Genia kept her maiden name, Kovarskaya, for her art. She had a studio of her own and she continued to work although Vilenski overshadowed her. I do not recall ever seeing her art but she was supposed to have had extremely good taste in what she did. Genia and Vilenski both had studios in a complex of ten or more large studios. One end of the studios was open so that lorries could drive in to transport the statues. Genia said we could not imagine what they had been through or the terrible things that had happened in the war but I said we had a very good idea. But nothing happened to them; they were evacuated during the war and besides, creative artists were always well rewarded and looked after in Soviet Russia. When Genia and her husband visited Paris, she was struck by the fact that everyone smiled. Russians take the view that they have nothing to smile about and go around with grimaces on their faces. She also said she was surprised that the shops did not go bankrupt. I asked her why and she said, "Because there are no queues!"

There is a lot to be said for Russian women. Someone once said, "If you haven't been loved by a Russian woman, you haven't lived." Genia was immensely sweet and immensely Russian. She was always terribly pleased to see me on my visits and asked me to meals that would go on for hours with dish after dish. She made these meals single-handed and only later with some help from her daughter Musia. She was not however very well informed about drink and was herself quite abstemious. Genia died soon after my last visit in May 1990. She was suffering from vertigo but otherwise she seemed all right when I saw her. She was very sorry to see me go and I think she said something about it being the last time we would see each other.

Musia was Genia's only child. She lived in Moscow while her husband lived in quite a large flat in Tbilisi where he was deputy to the chief architect. Now they live together near Moscow in a dacha they built themselves. She came top of her year in architecture, beating her husband, and she worked for a while for a young Jewish architect but after that she led a rather worldly life. She was, after all, a rich man's daughter because Vilenski had earned an enormous amount. Every time he churned out another bust of Lenin he got the equivalent of fifteen thousand pounds. He made statues of a wide range of people, all the academics and so on. In '66 he made a sculpture of Martyn which they wanted us to take back to England but it was only plaster so it was rather vulnerable. It finally reached England twenty-eight years later, brought out by one of Martyn's Russian friends. Musia's daughter, Nina, married Alyosha Novitskii, the son of a KGB general who was half-Georgian. The KGB general is now retired but was always harmless because he was on the information technology and communications side.

My mother had six half sisters. The eldest, Anna, married a successful financier called Socher. He was very neat, had a small Poincaré grey beard and a reputation for being extremely mean; after the Revolution he consulted people obsessively about the best places to hide jewels and gold coins. He was not well thought of by the family because his financial operations were not clear and he was even suspected of being a money-lender. However, he always gave me very good presents such as a telegraph machine on which you could type out messages on to tape.

Iliena, married Dr. Gregori Schmerling. They had three sons, Vladimir, Boris and Alexander who were all much older than me. Vladimir managed to get himself arrested by the Tsar's police for revolutionary activities while he was a student. After the Revolution he was promptly re-arrested by the Bolsheviks for being excessively right wing and eventually perished in a camp. Boris was involved in the food industry and I met him when I first went for dinner at Musia's flat, not so many years ago. He was a solidly-built man and although he was already in his mid-eighties, he went on eating and drinking for a good four hours. He drank three quarters of a bottle of strong vodka called *Starka* and at least a bottle and a half of Soviet champagne. This seemed to have no effect except perhaps in the slight eccentricity of raising his glass to my son Martyn and saying in Latin, "Let us have another glass!" At some point he married a real peasant woman who was not received in Genia's flat even in Soviet Russia. I was told, however, that she was extremely nice and Boris spent many years educating her, making her read decent books, taking her to museums and so on. The third son, was my handsome cousin Alexander who was killed in the First World War as an officer in the Medical Corps and whom I had admired in his officer's uniform as a young child.

Another half-sister, Rosa married a gynaecologist called Dr Krol. They lived in St Petersburg. He had an impressive appearance and was very tall with a small beard. She died quite young and I do not know whether they have any descendants. The fifth of Mother's half-sisters was married to a soap manufacturer called Grusd. He was a solidly built man with large features. His manners were not at all refined but his soap was splendid and compared favourably with the best Western products. My aunt and uncle never went hungry after the Revolution for although his factory was requisitioned, he was able to manufacture enough soap in their kitchen to exchange for food. They had two children, a boy called Grisha and a younger daughter who had a French governess. I learnt of Grisha's fate from the autobiography of an English journalist posted to Russia in the late 1930's. The journalist was trying to report on a balloon race but could not follow the balloons because all Westerners were restricted to a radius of forty kilometres from Moscow. However he discovered a society of radio amateurs of which my cousin Grisha was the secretary. The journalist approached Grisha and asked whether the various radio hams along the route could radio the arrival of the balloons to Moscow so that Grisha could relate the information to him. This venture began happily but in due course Grisha was arrested, presumably for spying for England, and dispatched to a camp.

When we were at the exhibition in '66, a man somewhat younger than me turned up and said that he was my cousin. His name was Viktor Poliakoff and he was the son of my Uncle Solomon in St Petersburg. Naturally, I asked him to dinner and I saw him on subsequent visits because he used to come over from Leningrad especially to see me. He was an electronics engineer in a defence establishment and so he had to get permission. Viktor talked about his elder half-brother, Vladimir who had come to stay with us in the dacha before we left Russia. Vladimir was slightly older than me and, at the time, we were both twelve or thirteen. He became the Soviet Union's leading satirical theatre and film writer, and the Head of Government had to approve all his films. "The Carnival Night", a skit on bureaucracy, was not allowed to be shown until Khrushchev had seen it and laughed so much he fell off his chair. From then on, the film was shown every New Year's day for sixteen years.

I wanted to meet Vladimir but Viktor said, "No. He's behaved dreadfully towards his aunt. He refused to visit her in hospital and said he had never heard of her." These were all lies. Eventually, my daughter Lucinda received a phone call while she was staying with Mouma's daughter Betka who was by then living in Russia with her husband, a journalist with the Agence France Press. A woman spoke to Lucinda in English and said, "Your father is my husband's aunt" (a slightly imperfect formulation) and left her telephone number. When I arrived in Moscow, I phoned and discovered that the woman was Vladimir's wife. Olga was thirty years younger than him and his sixth wife. I arranged to collect them and bring them to my suite at the Intourist Hotel. I gave the usual elaborate lunch with two waiters at either end of the table in smoking jackets, which was a novelty for the Soviets. Vladimir had never had wine approaching the quality of the Alsace wine I gave him. He was very likable, something of a playboy and immensely successful although by that time his popularity was beginning to wane. At one time, seventy-five theatres in the Soviet Republics were performing one of his plays simultaneously. We brought Vladimir and his wife to England for three weeks in '77 and took them to Cambridge and Scotland. Olga was mad on shopping of course. Vladimir died of cancer but I still keep in touch with Olga on the phone. She is not in a happy situation and now works in a government office although she did not have to work while Vladimir was alive.

A substantially younger brother of Uncle Vitia named Mulia was a nepman and I spoke to his widow on the telephone when I first went to Russia. That was when people were still frightened of foreigners so she did not seem at all keen for me to call on her. She probably lived in circumstances which she thought were too miserable for me to see. Except for very privileged people, flats were either communal or very tiny. But no one seemed to complain too much, unlike in Czechoslovakia where they complained like anything. Life for many Russians was much better then than it is now.

Father had three brothers: Solomon in St Petersburg, Naum and Boris. They were the last generation of Poliakoffs to be given Jewish names. Solomon was a big chap, taller than my father. He and his wife were dentists and, in the words of their son Vladimir, they drilled away in their flat for all they were worth. They lived in a six room flat, which was quite something for Soviet Russia, although it was in Leningrad not Moscow. Solomon and Vladimir came to stay with us in the country after the Revolution and when they left, Solomon gave me an extremely elaborate edition of Byron, translated into Russian, in several volumes with premium bindings – not an entirely appropriate present for a young boy. Naum, known to me as Uncle Nunia, was not successful. I think he read law at university but he never practised as a lawyer and my father tried to settle him in a job. At some point, Father found him a position on the railway but that did not last long. Then without any warning he turned up at the dacha with a wife. It was winter so how we found space to put them up I do not know. She was a provincial Jew and spoke Russian with a Yiddish accent. She wore a very showy Persian lamb coat and I heard my aunt say to my mother, "A disaster." Nunia survived indefinitely although I never met him on my Russian visits. My cousin Vladimir, kept in contact with him and by that time I think Nunia had a peasant wife. Nunia became an alcoholic in his old age and used to call on Vladimir for money to buy drink. He must have been approaching ninety, so it cannot have done him a lot of harm. The youngest brother Boris disappeared. My papa never showed the slightest curiosity as to what happened to him and I know next to nothing. I think he left Russia in a hurry, possibly for military service but it may have been for a less reputable reason, and he was supposed to have gone to America. There were some rumours that he had been spotted in Cuba and then the children met a lawyer who specialised in gangsters, with the same name as us, who could have been his grandson.

In the Ostankino hotel where we stayed on our first visit to Moscow in '66, you had to look for a seat in the restaurant, wait for someone to get up and then you sat for an age before they took the order. You waited again for an hour or more before you got any food. But gradually I discovered the way to do things in Moscow. You could travel to Soviet Russia on one of three tariffs: Deluxe, First Class or Business. If you travelled Deluxe class, the tariff included a car and driver for ten or twelve hours a day. So I used to insist that they sent me the biggest car they had which was called a *Chaika* (meaning seagull) instead of the standard Volga. Once I went in person to book a table at a restaurant. I arrived in my *Chaika*, saw the head waiter and explained the usual thing. "We have come from London and I'd like everything to be ready when we arrive." So when our car drove up in the evening, the manager was outside waiting for us and escorted us to our table.

I always tried to secure the best suite in a hotel, which cost no more than the worst suite, so that I could receive my Soviet guests there. Once when I was in Russia alone, I stayed in a suite in the new National Hotel which was on two floors. It had four rooms including a study and a dining room with an incredible rococo mirror and an elaborate candelabra. I also stayed in Suite 105 at the National Hotel which has the balcony from which Lenin had addressed the crowd. On another occasion, I held a party in suite 101, which houses Lenin's bed. Khrianin helped organise the party and acted as Master of Ceremonies. There was all the usual terrible extravagance which the Russians expect: hors d'oeuvre which lasts an hour and a half with black caviar, red caviar, smoked sturgeon, Russian salad (made with potatoes and called 'English salad' in Russia), gherkins and cold meats washed down with vodka, white and red French wine, champagne and brandy. The main course was pressed poussin. My guests included the head of the Moscow health service, the Moscow Head of Protocol and Pavlenko, the director of international exhibitions. After dinner, the Head of Protocol sat herself at the piano and played a few songs and a small collection of porters and others listened outside the door.

Eventually I was left, with my favourite waitress, to clear up. She said she had been worried about me having to drink so many toasts. We started shifting the furniture around when a dark young man I had never seen before appeared wearing an old Trinity College Cambridge tie. He had stayed in the suite on previous visits and wanted to know what was going on. So I said, "Well come on then, don't stand about, help us," and we started shifting the furniture. Then we talked a bit and after that we met twice, once with some rather dull Russians and once without. He was in partnership with his uncle and aunt who were wool merchants from Beirut.

When we were there in '66 I thought it might be amusing to go to the Prague, a very well known restaurant in Arbat Street, close to where we once lived. When we arrived at the restaurant, there was a queue at the door which was locked and on the other side of the glass door, stood the usual Tolstoy look-alike with the longish beard, very Russian features and headgear that looks like a chauffeur's cap but is not. I had only been in Russia for a short time so I hesitated but then two young women said to us, "Don't wait in the queue. Go to the door and knock." I learned later that foreigners did not queue. The only time one had to queue was if one wanted something to eat or drink during the interval at the Bolshoi Theatre. Then, everyone was a foreigner and one could not very well cut them. So I knocked on the door and Tolstoy opened it unwillingly. I asked, "Where's the Director?"

"First floor"

Ina and Martyn were waiting outside so I rushed up the stairs, burst into the office marked "Director" and said, "What's this? My father and grandfather used to come here and now you don't even let us in." He said, "Calm yourself, calm yourself. I'll see to it." So he came down and made Tolstoy let Ina and Martyn in. When we were all inside, I heard the girls, who had told me to knock, pleading with Tolstoy to let them in as well. He said, "Oh all right" and they went in.

Everything in Moscow was being used to more than its full capacity; buses, trams, theatres, bars. Only the metro was not so overloaded. All the restaurants were full. The fact that one had to wait so long that one ended up eating lunch at five o'clock did not seem to deter anybody. But people with foreign currency did not suffer in any way. The last time I was there we had dinner in the hard currency restaurant at the National and for the first time in my life, I could not finish my black caviar.

I went several times to a Georgian restaurant where they served unusual Georgian salads. On one occasion, two uninhibited young Georgians were there with two peroxide-blonde commercial girls to whom they paid no attention. The young men went quite wild and danced between the tables. One of the dances involved picking up their glass with their teeth, standing up and drinking from it. On another occasion, I went to the Slaviansky Bazar, the restaurant frequented by my Shabbat Grandfather. My Russian guest got drunk and was an embarrassment. There was a young waiter and a woman maître d'hôtel who crept up behind him and whispered, "SMILE."

We went to lunch at a restaurant in Arkhangeslkoye, in the country not very far from Moscow, on the estate of either Yosupov or Sheremetev. My friend Khrianin and his girlfriend had said they would like to be taken out to lunch there but said that I would have to book because they would only accept reservations from foreigners. So he gave me the phone number. I phoned and a man answered. I said, "I'd like a table for six for lunch tomorrow."

"Six of you? Tomorrow?"

"Yes."

"Well, what can I do about it?"

"What do you mean? You book it."

"Oh no, I can't"

"Why can't you?"

"Well, where's the book to write it in? The manager has it. And where's the manager? He's gone off. You phone tomorrow."

So I phoned the next day and this time a woman answered the phone. Men and women did alternate shifts. I said, "Here we are from London."

"How do I know you come from London? You speak perfectly good Russian."

I said, "Wait, we are staying at the Rossiya Hotel, this is our room number, this is our telephone number and we are coming to lunch tomorrow at one o'clock. Now you put the hors d'oeuvre on the table, vodka, white wine, red wine."

She said, "Don't worry, don't worry, everything will be all right, no need to worry."

So we arrived at a wooden-fronted estate house with a covered balcony on the first floor. The usual Tolstoy was guarding the door and I told him that we had booked a table. He said, "Please come in." Up the stairs we went and were led to a table the like of which I have never seen in spite of my frequent visits to Russia. Martyn took a photograph of it. There was too much of everything: black caviar, red caviar, flowers, wines, vodka. Khrianin was a tremendous eater but his girlfriend played the delicate young woman and perhaps expected him to persuade her but he was much too busy getting it down to pay her much attention. It was a very good lunch for Soviet Russia. Hors d'oeuvres were always good but the main courses were generally bad. We came in two cars, a hired Volga with imitation leopard skin covers and our regal red Rolls Royce which we had transported by sea from Tilbury to Leningrad. This was a very worthwhile venture. The Rolls stood outside the exhibition and everyone who saw it inquired which company it was with. We had a splendid driver, Alexander Petrovich, who was with us a fortnight and did not take any time off. At the end of our stay we gave him a superior fur hat which was what he said he wanted. At some point Khrianin drove the Rolls Royce and alarmed Alexander Petrovich terribly because he accelerated too much.

Russians on the whole are very easy going. They set out to like other people and expect other people to like them, an expectation which is of course not always justified. Moscow is like a large cocktail party. You talk to everybody in the hotel, the person who sits near you or the person who shares your table. No matter what nationality they are, if they are old Moscow hands they will talk. And in the service bureau you talk to the girls and get to know them. It is very touching how they remember you and try very hard for you. They tell you straight away where they went to university, what their ambitions are and whether they are married or not. Visitors to Moscow adopt the Russian attitude that everybody matters, that one might learn something and spread happiness around.

When I visited Russia in May 1990, no one was afraid any more. My driver told me that he had only been working for Intourist for a short period so I asked him what he had done before that. There was a long pause and then he said that he had been an officer in the KGB. Clearly he was not particularly proud of it. The drivers were obviously involved in all sorts of things, including supplying black market caviar, which I always resisted. And they tried things they would not have tried before. Thus I went to the car and found a young woman sitting next to the driver. So I said, "Who's that?" and he said, "I hope you don't mind. She's a chamber maid at the hotel." It was not clear whether, like the caviar, this was intended as another black market transaction. Anyway I was not pleased and it would have been unthinkable before.

Russians Abroad

Once, when I had been out to dinner in Paris, I called a taxi to take me back to my hotel. When the taxi arrived I was sure that the driver was Russian but when I asked, he said he was not. So I said, "All right, if you aren't Russian, what are you?" and he told me he was Czech. Then I asked where in Czechoslovakia he came from and he dithered so I thought he must be lying. After we had been driving for some time, he turned round and said, "I'm sorry. Of course I'm Russian but there are so many of us here that the Trade Union asks us not to tell."

We arrived at my hotel. By this point he was talking in the flowery language of the Caucasus. I took out a large note and he said, "Light of my heart, I am unable to change it." The porter was nowhere around so I proposed that we go and have a drink and then we would have some change. We went to a nearby bistro. I think the proprietor there was Russian as well. My taxi driver produced a photograph of himself as an officer in the Wild Division, dagger and all. He told me he was a Muslim and that his daughter was at the Sorbonne reading English and he wanted her to go to London. So I said, "That's not difficult to arrange" but then he told me he wanted a nice Muslim family and I grew more pessimistic.

When we returned to the hotel, it occurred to me that this was my last night in Paris and it did not do to go to bed at ten o'clock. So we set out again for a Russian night-club in Montmartre. When we arrived I said to the driver, "Come in" and he said, "Oh no. I'm not suitably dressed." So we argued for a bit and then I went in alone. I used to go to the Russian night-clubs quite frequently to listen to the gypsies. On this occasion, the first person I met was a male gypsy I knew who was also a Muslim. So I said to him, "Now go and get the other Muslim" which he did and then we sat down. One of the entraîneuse, a pleasant Soviet Russian girl sat down with us, and my driver had a thrilling time. He remembered that he was an officer and a gentleman and kissed her hand at frequent intervals and she sang. At four o'clock or thereabouts we decided it was time to go home and off we went. By this time the porter was standing outside the hotel, presumably concerned about what had happened to me. I got out and gave the taxi-driver a substantial note. He said, "No, light of my heart, I'm not taking any money from you." The porter could not have understood what was going on as we were speaking in Russian but he saw the opposite of the usual: me pushing the note and the driver rejecting it. Eventually however he accepted the money and went off.

On another trip to Paris, I went to a night-club which I had never been to before called La Chauve-Souris. It was also in Montmartre and they had a visiting Russian company called Baliv, which Ina and I had seen in London before the war, with light music and original sketches. I sat down by myself and the Russian proprietor came up and I invited him to sit down. His name was something like Finkelstein so I said, "Finkelstein where were you born?" He did not answer so I said, "Come on, come on where?" So he said, "Oh all right, Bilastok." Now, Bilastok crops up in jokes and remarks along the lines of, "What do you expect from him, he comes from Bilastok" So Finkelstein was defensive. He said, "Do you know that all the famous people were born in Bilastok?" I said, "No, I don't know" and he told me that Weizman, then President of Israel, was born in Bilastok. I had just read Weizman's autobiography so I knew that he was not born in Bilastok but in Pinsk. I said, "Wrong, he was born in Pinsk" And with a typically Jewish intonation and gesture he said, "And is it far from Bilastok to Pinsk?" The distance is about two thousand miles. When I was in Paris with Ina and our sons, I discovered that La Chauve-Souris had shut down and re-opened somewhere in the suburbs. Finkelstein was not doing very well and we went and had dinner there. It was a modest place but the Russian dishes were quite good.

When we were staying in Milan in the early 1970's, Ina discovered that there was a Russian restaurant not far from our hotel. At that time, there were controls on exporting money from England, although a lot of people cheated. The allowance for personal expenditure was twenty-five pounds in addition to which I had a modest business allowance. We went to the restaurant which was in a basement and immediately saw that it was grand-luxe with a vengeance. There were mounds of caviar and a multitude of waiters. I asked the maitre d'hôtel whether he spoke Russian and he said yes, he was Russian. So I explained that we had come from London and had an extremely small allowance; if the dinner was going to be very dear we had better go away. He said, "No, no. Let me call the proprietress." A good looking dark woman who turned out to be Armenian and spoke faultless Russian appeared and said, "Don't go. Guests are sent to us by God. Spend what you've got, we don't want anything more." So we sat down and two waiters appeared holding a bottle of vodka in the shape of a pyramid. I declined the vodka but she said, "It's on the house." So I had two or three glasses. We had a good dinner with red wine and then she asked us to her table and introduced her Italian husband and sang. When the bill came it was three pounds. So there is a certain advantage in coming from Russia.

It is now easier for me to speak to my Russian friends in English than in Russian. I have a Russian friend called Kiryl Fitzlyon Zinoviev and more often than not we speak to each other in English. His wife is English but learnt to speak perfect Russian with no accent and she runs the Russian

Refugee Aid Society, a house for old *babushkas* in Chiswick. But I still consider myself a Russian. We all do. One's childhood and boyhood cannot be written off, nor can one's parents. The Russians, like the Poles, kiss the hands of married women. When I came to England people on the whole did not kiss hands but like all the Russians I went out of my way to do so and still do. We keep up the Russian identity with a vengeance.

Alexander Poliakoff & Deborah Sacks
London, 1994